D0616125

BV 3790 .F633
Ford, Leighton.
Good news is for sharing

Leighton Ford

Good News is for Sharing

David C. Cook Publishing Co.

ELGIN, ILLINOIS—WESTON, ONTARIO
FULLERTON, CALIFORNIA

BV
3790
.F633

GOOD NEWS IS FOR SHARING

© 1977 David C. Cook Publishing Co.

All rights reserved. Except for brief excerpts for review purposes, no part of this book may be reproduced without written permission from the publisher.

Published by David C. Cook Publishing Co.
850 N. Grove Ave., Elgin, IL 60120.
Printed in the United States of America.

Fourth paperback printing, October 1982

Scripture quotations, unless otherwise noted, are from the New International Version.

The chart on page 86 is taken from *What's Gone Wrong with the Harvest?* by James Engel and H. Wilbert Norton. Copyright © 1975 by The Zondervan Corporation. Used by permission.

To Jeanie,
whose very life is good news shared

CONTENTS

Preface   ix
1   Have You Ever Tried to Ride a Lion?   1
2   I Found It—But Who Needs It?   12
3   Lost?   22
4   Does the Gospel Really Work?   37
5   Oh Where, Oh Where Is Stan Smith?   52
6   Let My People Grow   67
7   How the Good News Travels   85
8   The Bible and the Bullhorn   96
9   Building Bridges   104
10 Bridges Are for Traffic   116
11 Tell Me the Old, New Story   128
12 King James, Ken Taylor, and You   147
13 The Reasons Why   159
14 How to Be an Introducer   168
Postscript   How Do I Get Started?   183
Appendix   Questions, Questions   189

PREFACE

WE WERE IN the little Caribbean island of Grand Cayman for an evangelistic outreach. Just before an evening program, my wife discovered that her diamond engagement ring was missing. She bravely kept it to herself until the meeting was over, then told me that she feared she had dropped it on the beach.

Friends helped us search the motel and sift through the sand where she had been sitting earlier. There was no ring.

We went back to our room, crushed not just by the monetary loss but because so many loving memories were tied to that ring.

Then, under some papers on the bed, I found it! Gloom turned to joy! We hugged each other, said a prayer of thanks, and, although it was near midnight, I raced down the hall and knocked on our friends' door to tell them the good news!

Good news is like that—it begs to be shared. We Christians have both the responsibility and the privilege of passing on the good news that, through faith in Jesus Christ, eternal abundant life is offered to all people.

But why are we so often reluctant sharers? Why, even when we sometimes feel a strong sense of "oughtness" about witnessing, do we fail to do it?

I think there are several reasons:
- Fear of how people will react
- Not knowing how to communicate or what to say
- The belief that witnessing is "just not my gift"
- The lack of motivation
- A distorted view of what evangelism and witnessing involve

Some identify faith-sharing with a certain technique, program, or verbal pattern. Others associate it with high-pressure salesmanship. They find it difficult to get psyched up to something that seems unnatural.

I am so glad it doesn't have to be that way. Faith-sharing at its best comes from the overflow of a life shared with Jesus Christ and others on a day-by-day basis. I like the way Paul puts it:

"God . . . through Christ changed us from enemies into his friends and gave us the task of making others his friends also" (2 Cor. 5:18, Good News Bible).

Sharing good news is a life-style patterned after God. It is a life of making friends for God, as God has made us his friends through his Son.

How can we develop such a life-style? That's what *Good News Is for Sharing* is all about.

"How long did it take you to write this book?" someone asked.

"Forty-five years," I answered, tongue only partly in cheek. In a very real sense, this book has grown out of a lifetime of passing on the good news. I have tried to share both biblical truth and practical experience that God has given.

Denny Rydberg asked me to write this book, and I deeply appreciate him being the catalyst to get me started. I also must thank longtime friends and colleagues Irv Chambers, Norman Pell, and Ford Madison for talking over many of the ideas I've used. The thoughts of countless friends and writers have surely made their way into the manuscript. My wife, Jeanie, and our children, Debbie, Sandy, and Kevin, have been great sounding boards and sources for me. Jeanie read the proofs carefully and gave many helpful insights. Dean Merrill has been a skillful editor. And Jo Boynton typed the manuscript with a dedication that makes this her book, too!

Most of all, I pray that this may be the Lord's book, a tool to help all who read to share the only news that will grow better for all eternity.

I

Have You Ever Tried to Ride a Lion?

The Christmas our Kevin was nine, someone gave him a set of C. S. Lewis's Narnia books. Kevin read each of the seven books at least half a dozen times and he also got his daddy hooked. For over two years, we read Narnia together.

We started with The Lion, the Witch and the Wardrobe and were soon fascinated by the powerful and mysterious Aslan.

The mystical land that the children enter has been bewitched by the White Queen into a land of eternal winter. But it is rumored that a wonderful being named Aslan is coming to change everything. As the sense of Aslan's arrival increases, the land begins to brighten and the snow melts.

One day the children come face-to-face with him. To their wonder and amazement, he is a huge, golden lion. He looks both "good and terrible." In Aslan's presence, the grip of winter breaks, and the world becomes alive again.

After his conquest of the White Queen near the end of the book, Aslan gives a terrible roar and tells the children they have to go on a long journey with him. Climbing on his golden back, they grab his great tawny mane, and he shoots off faster than the fastest horse.

What a ride it must have been! C. S. Lewis

describes it: "Have you ever had a gallop on a horse? Think of that . . . then imagine instead . . . the soft roughness of golden fur, and the mane flying back in the wind . . . twice as fast as the fastest race-horse . . . a mount that doesn't need to be guided and never grows tired. He rushes on and on . . . threading his way with perfect skill between tree-trunks, jumping over brush and briar and the smaller streams, wading the larger, swimming the largest of all. And you are riding not on a road . . . but right across Narnia . . . through wild orchards . . . past roaring waterfalls . . . up windy slopes . . . across the shoulders of heathery mountains . . . and down, down, down again and into wild valleys and out into acres of blue flowers."[1]

Have you ever tried to ride a lion?

READ THE FOLLOWING LIST, and note what idea comes into your mind after each word.

Politics: _____ ?
Education: _____ ?
Sports: _____ ?
Journalism: _____ ?
Evangelism: _____ ?

When I did that word association test with a number of people, I found their image of evangelism varied widely.

Some associated it with a message: gospel, good news, salvation, born again.

Others identified it with a personality, usually Billy Graham.

Still others pictured evangelism as a method or approach: crowds, TV programs, the Four Spiritual Laws.

The most frequent and obvious association, however, was with Jesus Christ. Evangelism is something that believers in Jesus Christ practice.

But what is it?

You would think that everybody would agree on what evangelism is. The word itself is simple enough; it contains the word *evangel*, which literally means "good news." But what is the good news? How do we spread it? And what do we hope to achieve by it? Not all Christians give the same answers to these questions.

To some, evangelism simply means bringing individuals to a "decision for Christ." To others it means recruiting new members for the organized church. Still others speak of "evangelizing the structures of society," by which they mean changing government, education, and economic structures to bring about more justice. Even evangelical, biblical Christians are wrestling deeply with this issue.

So what is evangelism? Is it what Billy Graham does in a stadium? Is it what Martin Luther King did in the streets? Is it getting someone to hit the sawdust trail or "pray to receive Christ"? Is it changing individuals or changing the world?

If we believe in the authority of the Bible, we will likely turn to the Bible—and be surprised to find that it has no easy answer! The Bible doesn't even use the word *evangelism*. In fact, the word itself is relatively new. As far as we know, it didn't appear in English until about two hundred years ago.

Nor does the word *evangelist* occur often in the Bible. Philip the deacon was called an evangelist (Acts 21: 8), Timothy was told to "do the work of an evangelist" (2 Tim. 4: 5), and Paul describes the evangelist as one of the gifts Christ has given to the church (Eph. 4: 11).

However, the verb form of the word appears often in the New Testament. *Euaggelizo,* which basically means "to proclaim the good news," is used over fifty times. Angels were said to *evangelize* when they told the good news of Jesus' birth (Luke 2: 10). Jesus himself proclaimed *the evangel* of the Kingdom of God (Mark 1: 14). Paul said that he *evangelized* the people at Corinth (1 Cor. 15: 2).

By using verbs to talk about evangelism, the Bible puts the stress on *action*.

With that in mind, let me suggest that we start not with a definition but with an image of evangelism. What is it? *Evangelism is like riding the back of a lion.* This is evangelism, Aslan style!

Of course, Aslan is a symbol of Christ the Lion. God's dying-risen Lion-Lamb-Savior-Lord gave an awesome word to some frightened, doubting "children" on a lonely mountain: "All authority in heaven and on earth has been given to me. Therefore go and make disciples of all nations, baptizing them in the name of the Father and of the Son and of the Holy Spirit, and teaching them to obey everything I have commanded you. And surely I will be with you always, to the very end of the age" (Matt. 28: 18-20).

We have to grasp these basics if we are really to understand what evangelism is all about.

By what authority?

To start with, the authority of Jesus is the most basic fact in all of history to Christians. Jesus said, "All authority has been given to me." The early Christians responded by saying, "Jesus is Lord!" That was their brief summary of their faith.

It's highly important to be clear on what kind of authority Jesus claims. *Authority* in the ears of many people has a brittle, harsh, domineering sound. We rightly resent those who set themselves up as pompous, self-serving "authorities." And yet, paradoxically, our world is really hungry for true and genuine authority.

Authority was not something Jesus *imposed,* but something he *exposed.* Study the fourth through the ninth chapters of Matthew, and you will find several examples. He comes to some fishermen and simply says, "Follow me," and they do. He teaches his beautiful Sermon on the Mount, and everybody is amazed that he teaches "as one who had authority" (7: 29). He heals sicknesses, casts out evil spirits, calms a stormy sea—and people marvel at his authority. After all this, when he asks his disciples who he is, Peter answers, "You are the Christ, the Son of the Living God" (16: 16).

Yet this one who had so much authority came not to impose himself but to lay down his life for others on a cross, and then to take it up again. Jesus' authority is the authority of Aslan—both good and terrible. His authority is that of tough love, gentle strength. Jesus' authority exposed the truth that life is meant to run his way, God's way.

"Jesus is Lord," said the first Christians. But was he? Is he? Who is in charge of the world? Jesus? Man? Or the devil? Look at the lust and greed, the corruption and selfishness, the death and sickness around us.

A student in Australia once asked me, "Do you really believe that Jesus has all authority, when we live in a world like this?"

The answer is best given by an analogy. At present, the world is undergoing a change of administrations. Under democratic systems of government, elections are held regularly. If the incumbent retires or is defeated, there is a period when some may question who is in control. The old administration has been defeated but is still in power, though it is a lame-duck power. The new administration is not yet officially installed, but it begins to assume authority. The president- or prime minister-elect chooses his staff, begins to sort out his priorities, and makes statements on what his policies will be.

Since Jesus came the first time, the world has been "changing administrations." Jesus has won "all authority" by his death and resurrection, but he is not yet exercising that authority completely. Sin, death, evil, and the devil still have a little breathing space, a little time left. But though all do not realize it, Jesus *is* Lord, and when someday he comes back, every knee shall bow and every tongue confess that Jesus Christ is Lord, to the glory of God the Father!

Often people say, "Keep looking up." But the other day I did a double take when someone said, "Keep looking down." What he meant was that we who are in Christ ought to see life with *his* perspective. We already share in his present victory; we anticipate his final triumph. So we ought to be looking at the world and our own lives and the people around us with the perspective of Jesus Christ.

What does the authority of Jesus Christ have to do with you and me sharing our faith?

In the first place, it means that we Christians don't see ourselves as self-appointed saviors of the world. We aren't better than anyone else. We don't necessarily have more information. We aren't more clever than anyone else. We aren't any more confident in ourselves. We Christians share our faith because Jesus Christ is Lord. As an Asian Christian once said, we are "beggars telling other beggars where to get bread."

Other people may not see the authority of Jesus Christ. We have seen him; therefore we have to tell what we have seen. Paul put it this way, "The god of this age has blinded the minds of unbelievers, so that they cannot see the light of the gospel of the glory of Christ, who is the image of God. For we do not preach ourselves, but Jesus Christ as Lord, and ourselves as your servants for Jesus' sake" (2 Cor. 4: 4, 5).

The second thing Jesus' authority signifies is that sharing our faith is not an elective. It's a requirement. The Lord of all has "commanded us to preach to the people and to testify that he is the one whom God appointed as judge of the living and the dead" (Acts 10: 42).

The most basic question I have to ask as I think about sharing my faith is: "Who is in charge of my life? Is Jesus Christ really Lord?" His authority is more than that of a teacher who says, "Listen to what I say." His authority is more than a miracle worker who says, "Observe what I do." His authority is that of a Lord who says, "Follow me, and do what I say." How can I ask other people to make Jesus the center of their world if he's not the center of mine?

I will never forget landing at the airport in Dakar, West Africa. A missionary from France came out to meet us as we waited for our plane to refuel. We began to talk to him about his work and found that he had been in that Muslim area nearly ten years. Someone in our party asked him how many converts he had seen in that time, and he replied, "Two, maybe three."

Then someone thoughtlessly asked, "Well, why in the world do you stay here?"

He looked surprised and answered, "Why do I stay here? Jesus Christ put me here. That's why."

Toward what goal?

As Jesus' claim gives us our mandate, so his command gives us our aim in evangelism: "Therefore go and make disciples of all nations, baptizing them in the name of the Father and of the Son and of the Holy Spirit, and teaching them to obey everything I have commanded you."

It's especially interesting to find here only one imperative: "make disciples." Both *baptizing* and *teaching* are participles. A literal translation of this command might be, "Going, baptizing, and teaching—make disciples." The basic task of the church is to make disciples. Jesus Christ has not called us primarily to hold programs or give speeches or put up buildings or plan meetings (though all these may be necessary). The specific command Jesus gives us here is to *make disciples*—people whose lives reflect the glory of God and the character of Jesus Christ.

By focusing on disciple-making as the aim of evangelism, we find a practical solution to a question debated among Christian theologians and strategists: When is a person evangelized?

Is it when he has heard the gospel?

Is it when he has understood the gospel well enough to make an intelligent response?

Is it when he has "decided for Christ"?

Is it when he is baptized and identifies himself with a local church?

Or is it when he has learned the teachings of Christ and reached a point of maturity?

Some scholars hold to a very precise definition of *evangelism*. They say that the verb *to evangelize* in the Bible simply means "to proclaim the good news" and doesn't necessarily imply any response. To a degree, they are correct.

But others argue that we must give a broader definition. They point out that on almost every occasion when the word is used in the Book of Acts, the context indicates that there was a response to the gospel. Therefore they say evangelism means not only *proclaiming* the gospel but also *persuading* men to respond to it. The Covenant made at the historic Lausanne Congress on World Evangelization in 1974 asserts that "evangelism itself is the proclamation of the historical, biblical Christ as Saviour and Lord, with a view to persuading people to come to him personally and so be reconciled to God."

In either case we *can* agree that the command Jesus gives us in the Great Commission is crystal-clear. He tells us to "make disciples." We cannot simply tell people about Christ without caring whether or not they respond. Neither are we permitted to use any method to manipulate them. We are to care passionately and deeply and guide them into full discipleship.

To think of evangelism in terms of making disciples is helpful in avoiding another misunderstanding. Evangelism for many people is a kind of elite activity. They picture an *evangelist* as someone who is sent or goes some place special (another country, another city, another neighborhood). The evangelist engages in *evangelism* (a special kind of ministry, often involving some kind of public speaking). He does this to *evangelize* people, bringing them to a decisive moment or turning point in their lives.

Now all of this is true and important. There *are* people who are called by God to be evangelists in a special sense. They *are* sent to other places. They *do* perform unique ministries. And coming to Christ for many people *does* involve a decisive experience. But if we merely delegate sharing our faith to special people, special times, special places, and special events, then that lets us "normal people" off the hook. We may think, "That's something we don't have to do."

I don't believe that every Christian is called to be an evangelist in the specialized sense. But I do believe the biblical pattern is for everyone to be involved in a life-style of making disciples. A young man wrote recently saying, "I believe one of the main reasons Christians don't share their faith is that they just don't think of doing it when they have the opportunity." In other words, it is not a natural part of their lives.

Whatever term you may prefer to use—evangelizing, sharing your faith, communicating the good news, or making disciples—what is involved is not just an isolated event but a continuous process by which people are brought to Christ.

A quick glance at how the New Testament uses the word *disciple* will bring this out. Basically the word means a learner—one who accepts the teacher's beliefs and life-style. The word is used in many different ways in the New Testament. In a general sense, we read of the *disciples* of John the Baptist. Even in relation to Jesus, the word *disciple* is used in several senses. One day when Jesus gave a particularly hard saying, "many of his disciples turned back and no longer followed him" (John 6: 66). They were followers of Jesus, but they were not genuinely committed to him. So the word can be used of all followers of Jesus regardless of their commitment.

In the Book of Acts, *disciple* is used simply as a synonym of *Christian*. For example, "The disciples were first called Christians at Antioch" (Acts 11: 26). On other occasions, the word implies a marked degree of maturity in Christian growth. In this sense, *disciple* refers only to a dedicated, steady, loving, obedient, and fruitful follower of Jesus (Luke 14: 25; John 8: 31; John 13: 34, 35; John 15: 8).

Discipleship is not a point someone reaches. Rather, it is a process. I am a disciple if I am one who is moving with Jesus and for Jesus, learning from him, reaching out to others because of him.

Since making disciples is a process, each of us may play a different part in a person's coming to Jesus Christ. Translating the Great Commission just a bit differently will illustrate this. Ordinarily we think of Jesus as saying, "Therefore *go* and make disciples." Then we reason, "Well, I can't go," or "I haven't been called to go." In our minds we picture getting on a plane and going some place on the other side of the world.

But what the Great Commission is actually saying is *"As you go . . .* make disciples." Not all of us will be called to "go" overseas. But all of us can make disciples "as we go" in the normal traffic patterns of our lives, conscious of three things about every person we meet: God loves him, he has a need for God, and we can help him to take the next step toward God.

How do we do that? That's what this book is about. We make disciples by telling the story of Jesus Christ. We make disciples by discovering and using the unique gifts God has given each of us. We make disciples by loving, by demonstrating the reality of what we talk about, by the way we relate to other Christians. We make disciples by living his Word, modeling in our life-style the reality of the Kingdom of God. By our words, our gifts, our love, and our actions, we proclaim the good news and invite men and women to respond to Jesus Christ, to accept him as Savior, to follow him as Lord, to identify with his Body the Church, to do all things that he has commanded.

There once were two churches that stood across the street from each other. One was a very evangelistic church that concentrated on winning people to Christ. The other was a socially active church, very concerned about justice, civil rights, and helping the poor. The pastors used to snipe at each other regularly. One day the pastor of the evangelistically oriented church put a sign up on his lawn that said, "A body without a spirit is a corpse." The activist pastor countered with his own sign: "A spirit without a body is a spook."

Jesus Christ is not calling us to produce either corpses or spooks. He is calling us to make disciples, persons in whom the face of Jesus Christ will be fleshed out in the totality of their human lives.

When people commit themselves to Christ, they are committing themselves to Christ personally, to his Body, to his teachings, and to serve others for his sake. We should be evangelizing people so that they might become disciples who will live to the glory of God.

Will we succeed?

Jesus Christ gives us the promise that meets our most basic need. "Surely I will be with you always," he says, "to the very end of the age."

Roland Allen, a famous missionary thinker, explained that "the promised presence of Christ is not a reward offered those who obey, but rather the assurance that those commanded will be able to obey." One of the most common misunderstandings of evangelism is that it's something *we do* for Jesus Christ. But if I understand what Jesus is saying to us here, he is telling us that evangelism is something he does through us. It's not that Jesus Christ is saying, "Hey, you go out into the world there and do something for me." He is saying, "As you go through your life, through the struggles, the pains, the joys—to school, to work, to play, I am with you and I am working through you. I am making my authority known in all the earth. You trust me. You obey me, and I will be with you, and you will see that it is going to happen."

It is tremendously important to get this into our heads. Sharing the good news is *God's* mission. Evangelism is his work. At the very beginning of his ministry Jesus said, "The Spirit of the Lord is upon me." There you have the Trinity: the Lord (Father), the Spirit, and the Son. God is working out his plan in the world, sovereignly working all things according to his purpose. His purpose is to establish his Kingdom, to build his Body the Church, to make disciples. In order to carry this out, all authority has been given to Jesus Christ. The Holy Spirit is the one who empowers the Body of Christ. The Holy Spirit is the one through whom Jesus Christ carries out his work and the Father's purpose through the Church. Evangelism is not just a *commission* that God gives to us. It is a *co-mission.*

When we share our faith, we are actually working in partnership with the triune God.

Understanding this frees me from many of my hang-ups and

problems. It frees me from laziness and unconcern. How can I sit back and not care, when the living God, the Creator himself, is actually calling me to be a partner with him in the greatest work in the world! It frees me from pride, the haughty arrogance that turns more people away from Christ than it draws to him. It saves me from the fear of failure and despair. I don't let the fear of failure keep me from sharing my faith, nor do I let it lead me to manipulate people in a dishonest way so that I can get "results." I can be concerned for results, but I can leave people in God's hands, because this is his work, and he is doing it with me and through me. As writer/lecturer Ann Kiemel says, "God and love and I are out to change the world. I may be just an ordinary, everyday young woman, but in little ways everyday I am going to make a difference. You wait, you'll see."

This is the kind of evangelism to which Jesus Christ is calling you and me.

Jesus—Aslan—the mighty Christ, the moving Christ, the mysterious Christ is saying, "Get on my back—let's go for a ride—let's make some new Aslan people. Just hang on, and let's get going!"

1. C. S. Lewis, *The Lion, the Witch and the Wardrobe* (New York: Macmillan, 1951), p. 162.

2

I Found It—
But Who Needs It?

Several years ago I was with Billy Graham at the University of Tennessee. One night a large group of demonstrators came to the football stadium where he was speaking to boo and jeer.

When Billy gave the invitation to publicly accept Christ, one of them came forward, a long-haired, bearded guy wearing sandals. He stood at the front and raised both arms above his head. With one he gave the one-way sign for Jesus; with the other he gave the two-finger peace sign.

His response intrigued me, and I went over to talk with him. He told me that he had been involved in some very radical movements. He said he really wanted to see peace and justice in the world but now realized that Jesus Christ was the only way for this to happen, for him and for others. He lived in a house just off campus with several other radicals and asked if I would come over and talk that night.

I didn't particularly want to; I knew it would probably be rough. I quickly thought of other things I needed to do that night . . . but inside, I knew I was just chicken. So in the end, I agreed to meet them at a certain time.

Two friends agreed to go with me for moral

support! Finally, I went back to my room and prayed until the appointed time.

We had one of the most interesting evenings I have ever spent. We faced a lot of prejudice against the crusade and a lot of preconceived notions about Christianity, but basically these people were glad we came. They served some of their best food as we sat on the front porch and talked. We enjoyed a very deep discussion. And I think we were able to show them a picture of Jesus Christ, without the cultural imagery, that made sense and got many thinking about him.

But apart from the witness we gave, something happened to me. I found a new confidence and excitement in the gospel. I had been going through a period of some real doubt and testing and found some of this was overcome by seeing the gospel stand up in that kind of encounter. I wouldn't have missed that night for anything . . . but I almost did!

I AM AN EVANGELIST. Since I was fourteen years old I have been involved in witnessing and sharing my faith. I have preached to crowds of up to sixty thousand. And yet, many times I get more nervous talking about Christ to one individual in a situation that is not controlled and "safe" than I do talking to a crowd, where I pretty well know how things are going to go and what I'm going to say.

Fear needs to be dealt with right here in the second chapter. Because most of us are afraid for one reason or another.

To a certain extent, fear is normal. In fact, anyone who doesn't have a bit of apprehension might not be an effective communicator. Many times I have asked counselors being trained to talk to people who make a public response in our evangelistic meetings how many of them are scared. That usually draws a nervous chuckle, and most of them put up their hands. Then I tell them, "If you weren't a bit afraid, I don't think you would be qualified to be a counselor." It's easy enough to talk about the weather, sports, and casual things that don't matter much. But the more deeply we feel something and the more personal and sensitive it is, the more reluctant we may be to talk about it.

There is nothing more important than one's eternal relationship with God. If we have no hesitation in discussing this, then perhaps we don't understand how important and sensitive the issue is. It's only when we realize we are not sufficient to do the communicating that we can really be useful to the Lord.

Fear does not disqualify us from sharing our faith. If it did, the apostle Peter would never have made it. He was the man who was so afraid even to admit that he knew Jesus Christ that he denied it three times in one night. But he was also the man who preached the great evangelistic message on the Day of Pentecost, when three thousand people were converted.

Paul revealed to the Christian brothers and sisters in Corinth a side of himself that perhaps none of them had realized: "I came to you in weakness and fear, and with much trembling." But that fear led him to put his confidence even more in God and his Word. "My message and my preaching were not with wise and persuasive words, but with a demonstration of the Spirit's power, so that your faith might not rest on men's wisdom, but on God's power" (1 Cor. 2: 3-5).

Scottish Christian and scholar James Denney once said, "No man at one and the same time can show that he himself is clever and that Jesus Christ is mighty to save." Fear can be a good thing when it leads us to have a strong confidence in God, not in ourselves.

Sharing our faith, especially in situations where we don't have full control, can be risky and scary. Exposing ourselves to the unknown, risking failure, making ourselves vulnerable to the criticism or ridicule of others can be intimidating. And yet, I have found that some of my most exciting times as a Christian have been in these uncontrolled situations. Often I have walked into a rap session with a group of students or have gone onto a call-in radio program where I know it's "open season" on evangelists—and I've been scared. But I've prayed for the Lord to give me wisdom, and once we get going, the spiritual adrenaline seems to flow, and I find tremendous confidence and exhilaration, realizing that the gospel message is sound. It rings true. A faith that isn't risky, that is not worth betting our life on, just doesn't have the ring of reality.

In preparing for this book, I have talked to a lot of people, and the fear issue comes up front again and again. What makes people hesitate to share their faith? Here are some of the fears that have been mentioned to me:

- "I am afraid I might do more harm than good."
- "I don't know what to say."
- "I may not be able to give snappy answers to tricky questions."
- "I may seem bigoted."
- "I may invade someone's privacy."
- "I am afraid I might fail."
- "I am afraid I might be a hypocrite."

Perhaps the most common fear, however, is that of being rejected. A survey was given to those attending training sessions for the Billy Graham crusade in Detroit. One question asked, "What is your greatest hindrance in witnessing?"

Nine percent said they were too busy to remember to do it.

Twenty-eight percent felt the lack of real information to share.

None said they didn't really care.

Twelve percent said their own lives were not speaking as they should.

But by far the largest group were the 51 percent whose biggest problem was the fear of how the other person would react! None of us likes to be rejected, ridiculed, or regarded as an oddball. So how do we handle this fear?

Why we're afraid

It may help if we see that this fear has both a real and an imaginary basis.

Rejection by others is a real possibility when we share our faith. In fact, this possibility is implied in the very word *witness*, which in the Greek is *marturia,* the root of our word *martyr.* An authentic witness always carries the seed of the martyr. Rejection and ridicule are perhaps not as probable in North America now as a few years ago. And it's certainly less of a risk in the Western world than in communist-dominated countries or the Third World. Those of us who live in the West don't face much possibility of imprisonment or actual physical torture, though that may come someday. If we stand up for Jesus Christ, however, we still may be thrown to the lions of social pressure, intellectual jibes, and possibly even the loss of job opportunities.

Jesus made it rather clear that if we are going to follow him, we ought to expect some rejection. After all, he was "despised and rejected of men" (Isa. 53: 3). He "came to that which was his own, but his own did not receive him" (John 1: 11). And he said that the servant couldn't expect to be better than his master. "If the world hates you, keep in mind that it hated me first," he said (John 15: 18). We are soldiers involved in a life-and-death struggle with evil, and we have to expect some hardship. The question is, am I committed enough to Jesus Christ to be willing to let people know that I am a Christian, even if I have to lose some friends or social standing?

From boyhood, one of my favorite stories has been the forty martyrs of Sebaste. These forty soldiers, all Christians, were members of the famed Twelfth Legion of Rome's imperial army. One day their captain told them Emperor Licinius had sent out an edict that all soldiers were to offer sacrifice to the pagan gods. These Christians replied, "You can have our armor and even our bodies, but our hearts' allegiance belongs to Jesus Christ."

It was midwinter of A.D. 320, and the captain had them marched onto a nearby frozen lake. He stripped them of their clothes and said they would either die or renounce Christ. Throughout the night these men huddled together singing their song, "Forty martyrs for Christ." One by one the temperature took its toll and they fell to the ice.

At last there was only one man left. He lost courage and stumbled to the shore, where he renounced Christ. The officer of the guards had been watching all this. Unknown to the others, he had secretly come to believe in Christ. When he saw this last man break rank, he walked out onto the ice, threw off his clothes, and confessed that he also was a Christian.

When the sun rose the next morning, there were forty bodies of soldiers who had fought to the death for Christ.

Those men were not ashamed of Jesus Christ. But what about you and me? Paul said, "In fact, everyone who wants to live a godly life in Jesus Christ will be persecuted" (2 Tim. 3: 12). We are not told to invite it, or to provoke it, or to enjoy it—but we are told to expect it. What we have to understand is that this is not a personal rejection; it comes from being identified with Jesus Christ. He went through it, so did the apostles, and so have thousands of Christians through the centuries. If we face some ridicule and rejection, it's nothing compared to what they went through. As the writer of Hebrews said, "You have not yet resisted to the point of shedding your blood" (12:4).

So when I face the possibility of real opposition, the question is, will I obey Jesus Christ? If we acknowledge Christ, he will acknowledge us, he said. If we are ashamed of him, he'll be ashamed of us.

At a recent convention of Canadian psychiatrists, the president gave an address in which he expressed very strongly his Christian convictions. Afterwards, a friend of mine went up and mentioned that it must have taken a lot of courage to make those comments in front of a group containing many skeptics. "Courage?" the man answered. "No, it didn't really take courage. How could I ever face Jesus Christ if I were not willing to speak about him?"

When we face real opposition, all of us will sense fear. But are we going to let fear (and pride) rule our lives? Or are we going to let Jesus Christ rule? The opposite of courage is not fear but cowardice. Recently, I heard of a grad student who was a Christian but was afraid of what his intellectual friends might think of his faith. When some of them came for a get-together at his parents' home, he hid all the Christian magazines and Bibles and replaced them with secular magazines. What is that but sheer cowardice, not being honest enough to admit what he really is? Courage is just fear that has said its prayers—it's faith that has taken up its cross.

Are they *really* hostile?

On the other hand, some of our fear of people's reactions is based on false assumptions. We are afraid that people will reject us because they are not interested. This is a particular problem for those who have been brought up (as I was) in a strong, church-related, Christian environment. Often we've had minimum contact with non-Christians. Then when we get to know people and talk to them about Christ, we see that many of them are very, very interested.

Most people are turned off by the person who buttonholes them with the "Brother, are you saved?" approach (although

God can use that sometimes, too!). But I find that almost
everyone I have ever talked with has been willing and often
eager to talk about spiritual things if he can do it in a relaxed,
nonthreatening situation.

Some people are hardened to the gospel, and others express
no sense of need whatever. They are like the hard ground in the
parable of the soils, unplowed soil that the seed just bounces off.
In these cases, our job isn't to sell something they see no need
for. We have to take another approach, or just wait patiently
and prayerfully until God uses his plow to open their lives to the
gospel.

We should not assume, however, that people who say they
have no need really don't. We recently finished a two-year
interchurch evangelistic project in Vancouver, one of the most
secular cities in North America. Less than 20 percent of the
people attend church regularly. An attitude survey in the community showed that over 60 percent were satisfied with life as it
was—especially those in their twenties and early thirties.

Yet I was asked to go on an open-line radio program on a
youth-oriented station to discuss the topic, "What does religion
mean in your life today?" We were flooded with calls for two
hours. People wanted to share what religion meant in their lives.
Others called to discuss openly the hang-ups and objections
they had. The switchboard got so jammed with incoming calls at
one point that people were asking the station's operator to
explain what it meant to be born again!

Our task is not so much to create a sense of need in people's
lives as to uncover the need where God has already made it
known. A lot of our fear will disappear when we realize there are
people around us who are just waiting for someone to connect
with them, to share a faith that makes sense. God is often
already at work in the lives of those we speak to.

Paul says in Romans that God is already speaking, even to
pagans who do not have the Bible. He speaks to them through
creation, which clearly shows God's eternal power and divine
nature, testifying that this "whole show" didn't just happen out
of nothing (Rom. 1:20). He also speaks through conscience,
that moral stop-and-go light inside us, so that even people "who
do not have the law, do by nature things required by the law"
(Rom. 2:14).

Pretend you are living in the following situation. You are in a country where Christians are a distinct minority. The official policy is anti-Christian; in fact, a systematic program of harassment, imprisonment, torture, and in some cases even execution is being carried out against believers. To complicate the situation, your country has recently lost a war and is living under an occupying force of foreign troops. This foreign power is theoretically neutral about religion, but is actually worried that the Christian minority may destabilize the situation. Economically, you, like most other Christians, are definitely lower-class, with no political or economic clout.

Now, as if just surviving weren't enough, the leader of the little team of Christians announces that you are going on a visitation evangelism program. He hands you three names to choose from. You read the names, and almost fall over.

Number one is the secretary of the treasury of a powerful neighboring country. He has been visiting your capital for an economic conference. Number two is a leading official of the majority religion in your country, the man who is chiefly responsible for the campaign against Christians. Number three is one of the top officers of the occupying forces, a man known as a fair but tough administrator of the law.

Which would you choose?

If it were me, I think I'd turn in my evangelism badge right there!

But now look at the Book of Acts for a moment. We have almost the exact situation described above.

In Acts 8, the Lord ordered a Christian, Philip, to go down into the Gaza Strip and meet an important government official from Ethiopia who was sitting in his chariot and reading. I'm sure Philip must have been reluctant. But when he got there, he found that this man was actually reading the Book of Isaiah from the Old Testament and was trying to figure out whom the prophet was talking about. When Philip identified the subject of the passage as Jesus Christ, the man believed and was baptized on the spot!

In Acts 9, a man named Ananias had an even scarier assignment. The Lord said, "Go to the house of Judas on Straight Street and ask for a man from Tarsus named Saul" (v. 11). Ananias knew Saul's main priority was harassing Christians. But he went. When he got there, he found that Jesus Christ had already met Saul on the road to Damascus. Saul was waiting for someone to come and fill in the details about Jesus and tell him what to do next.

In Acts 10, the Lord told Peter to go to a Gentile army officer named Cornelius. Peter was so skeptical that God had to send a vision to convince him. Imagine the cultural gap. For a humble Jewish fisherman to go to the home of a leading Gentile army officer must have been a frightening affair. But again, when he got there, he found that Cornelius and all of his house had assembled and were waiting to hear Peter's message.

In all of these instances, God was there, opening the door before his people arrived. We ought to expect that God will do this today.

During the Montreal Olympics I met a French-Canadian girl whose story sounded like an incident in the Book of Acts. She had been seeing a psychiatrist who had told her to start sleeping with a lot of different men to get over her problems. She took his advice but found she was digging herself into deeper and deeper depression. Then she met a group of Hare Krishna people on the street in Montreal. When they tried to win her to their beliefs, she became extremely confused and decided to find out what she did believe about God. She went into a bookstore, picked up a book about Jesus, and sat down on a park bench to read it, praying that if God could really communicate he would show her the truth.

Only a few minutes later, two young people from Kansas who were part of a witnessing team at the Olympics came walking into the park, saw her sitting there, and felt impelled to go over and talk with her. They asked her if she would be interested in learning about Jesus! In the conversation they led her to an understanding of who Jesus Christ was, and she opened her life to him right there. Later I had the privilege of talking with her personally and seeing the transformation that took place in her life.

Now, of course, these are dramatic stories. Most of us don't see this kind of thing happen often—but we probably would if we were more sensitive and expectant about the leading of the Holy Spirit.

Certainly it's true that a few people we run into may be

hostile. A large number may be indifferent. But a lot of our fear that people are going to reject us and react negatively is just a preconceived idea in our minds.

The fact is that most people, if approached in a natural and sensitive way, will react with politeness and interest. Surprisingly, many have been waiting for someone to come. The way God has prepared them may not be as dramatic as Saul of Tarsus. But there are many persons around us who are dealt with through loneliness, bereavement, family crisis, sickness, concern about the world, search for purpose, or the need for forgiveness. Much of our fear will be gone if we realize that God will often lead us to those whose hearts he is ready to open.

The best antidote to fear is love—a love that leads us to forget our own fears and focus on the needs of others. Perhaps that's why Paul wrote to Timothy, apparently a sometimes hesitant type, to remind him that "God did not give us a spirit of timidity, but a spirit of power, of love, and of self-discipline" (2 Tim. 1: 7).

God's love will not only cast out fear; it will transform our witnessing from compulsion to compassion.

3

Lost?

My little girl was lost.

The certainty hit me, and I fought to keep panic away, to keep my mind clear as I reviewed the facts.

An hour and a half before, Debbie Jean had walked home from school. Thirty minutes ago, after a brief nap, she had gone out to play in the bright spring sun with her four-year-old brother Sandy. My wife had left me with the children while she went to the store, and for some time I worked in my study upstairs. Then when I called Debbie Jean to come in, there was no answer. Sandy told me she had gone back to school. This surprised me—although Sharon School was only a few hundred yards away, across some open fields and backyards, she seldom went there to play, and never without permission.

I went to look for her in the schoolyard, but she was not there. My wife drove up as I came back home. A little uneasy, we quickly checked the five other houses on our street; she was not at any of them. A neighbor's child said he had seen her go toward school. The mute lady who lived behind us confirmed by signs that she had indeed gone through her yard. Again I walked to the school, but some children playing there had not seen her.

While my wife checked the shopping center across the street, the principal and I went through the classrooms. There was no sign of her. Now I stood on a little-used dirt road between the rear of the school and our house. I looked at the woods. It was hard to push out of my mind stories I had heard of men picking up little girls. Should we call the police? Or was there any other place she might have gone? I walked up and down the road calling "Debbie Jean," fearing the silence.

Half an hour later our little girl came walking around a corner of the school, smiling. The explanation was simple but hard to take. She had gone to a candy store just beyond the school, met a friend, and gone on to her home a half mile away.

Later (when the thunder and lightning and tears were over!) I reflected on the incident. During the nearly two hours that Debbie Jean was missing, nothing else mattered. In my study were books to be read, letters to be answered, articles to be written, planning to be done—but it was all forgotten. I could think of only one thing: my girl was lost. I had only one prayer, and I prayed it a thousand times, "O God, help me to find her."

But how often, I asked myself, had I felt that same terrible urgency about people who were lost from God?[1]

As THE SUN SETS over the town of Capernaum, a man coming home from his day's work senses confusion and excitement in the streets. Everybody is running. He reaches out and grabs a friend by the robe. "What's going on?" he asks.

The man answers, "Jesus is here—Jesus of Nazareth—and he's preaching at Peter's house!"

The worker's eyes grow wide. He throws down his tools and breaks into a run, only he heads in the opposite direction from the crowd. He goes to the home of a friend, and the two of them go to the home of a third, and the three of them to a fourth. Then they go to a shabby little house where one of their friends

A portion of this chapter appeared in *Christ the Liberator* (Downers Grove, Ill.: InterVarsity, 1971), pp. 229ff.

lives. This man has been sick, paralyzed for years. They tell him, with their eyes shining, "Jesus is here—you know, the preacher, the prophet, the one who has healed so many people. He might be able to heal you. How about letting us take you to him?"

The man nods, and they each pick up a corner of the pallet on which he is lying. Running, hurrying, stumbling, they carry him until they get to the street where Peter's house stands. Imagine their disappointment as they look at the scene. The room where Jesus teaches is jammed full; the door and the courtyard are packed. Hundreds of people are milling around: there is no way for one person to get through that crowd, let alone four men carrying a stretcher.

Then one of them has an idea. "Why don't we take him up onto the roof and drop him through to Jesus?" In those days the roofs were flat, with staircases going up the outside, so this would be a fairly simple engineering matter.

None of the four said, "Well, I'm too busy. This is taking more time than I've got." No one said, "Wait a minute. First you tell me, who's going to pay for that roof?" None of them were diehard traditionalists who would say, "Take him through the roof? We can't do that—it's never been done before!" They simply looked at their own strong limbs and the hope dying in their friend's eyes, and they headed up the stairs and onto the roof.

I have been interrupted while speaking by babies, birds, and bugs, but I doubt if many preachers have literally had the roof raised over their heads. Jesus was in the midst of talking when suddenly the tiles in the ceiling were removed, and these four men lowered their friend in front of Jesus.

The story tells us that "when Jesus saw *their faith*" (they exercised faith on behalf of their friend), "he said to the paralytic, 'Son, your sins are forgiven' " (Mark 2: 5). The crowd stirred. Everybody expected him to say, "You are healed." Instead, he said, "You are forgiven."

Some of the teachers of the law were there thinking to themselves, "Why does this fellow talk like that? He's blaspheming! Who can forgive sins but God alone?" (v. 7).

Immediately Jesus sensed this, so he said to them, "Why are you thinking these things? Which is easier: to say to the paralytic, 'Your sins are forgiven,' or to say, 'Get up, take your mat and walk'?" (v. 9).

Nobody could see the forgiveness of sins, but everybody could see whether he actually got up and walked.

Then Jesus said, "That you may know that the Son of man has authority on earth to forgive sins . . . " and he told the paralytic, "Get up, take your mat and go home" (vs. 10-11).

The man "got up, took his mat, and walked out in full view of them all. This amazed everyone and they praised God, saying, 'We have never seen anything like this!' " (v. 12).

This is a case study of evangelism in action. Whenever we have true evangelism, we have the same cast of characters. There is a needy person. There is the Savior with his power to heal. And there are friends who care enough to link the person in his paralysis to Jesus and his power.

When you and I are missing links, it is usually because our understanding is insufficient at one of these points: human need, Jesus' power, or our responsibility.

Evangelism is costly work. One of my friends says, "Whenever anybody comes to Jesus, someone usually has to pay for the roof." The sharing of our faith with someone else often involves significant sacrifice.

Who cares?

The reason many of us don't witness is apathy. This is the big brother to the problem of motivation. We may say, "I don't have time," or offer some other excuse. But if we were pressed to give an honest reply, we would often have to say, "I just do not care enough that people are bound for an eternity without God." Because sharing our faith is costly—in terms of time, loving other people, giving ourselves, and being vulnerable— we are not likely to become involved unless we have deep convictions about the power and adequacy of Jesus Christ, about our own responsibility, and about the need of other people.

In his book *Evangelism in the Early Church,* Canon Michael Green of England discusses the evangelistic motives of the first Christians. It is interesting that he lists these same categories.

First, says Green, they were moved by a *sense of gratitude,* "the overwhelming experience of the love of God which they had received through Jesus Christ. The discovery that the ultimate force in the universe was Love, and that this love had stooped to the very nadir of self-abasement for human good, had an effect on those who believed it which nothing could remove."[2]

Again and again this sense of awe and gratitude appears in the New Testament. "I live by faith in the Son of God, who loved me and gave himself for me," said Paul (Gal. 2:20). "Since God so loved us, we also ought to love one another," wrote John. We witness because "we have seen and testify that the Father has sent his Son to be the Savior of the world" (1 John 4:11, 14). The sharing of our faith springs first of all from knowing who God is and what he has done for us through the life, death, and resurrection of Jesus Christ. These first Christians were moved by the example of a God who gave his Son and a Savior who gave his life.

The second main motive, according to Green, was a *sense of responsibility*. Paul wrote that "we make it our goal to please him, whether we are at home in the body or away from it. For we must all appear before the judgment seat of Christ, that each one may receive what is due him for the things done while in the body, whether good or bad" (2 Cor. 5:9, 10).

Paul did not fear, and neither need we fear, the final verdict of the Last Day. No condemnation awaits those who are in Christ. So, as Green points out, "This fear of which he [Paul] speaks is not the craven fear of the underdog, but the loving fear of the friend and trusted servant who dreads disappointing his beloved master."[3]

In his sovereign self-limitation, God's power is restrained by his own choice. God "has committed to us the message of reconciliation. We are therefore Christ's ambassadors, as though God were making his appeal through us" (2 Cor. 5:19, 20).

Jesus was born in a borrowed manger, he preached from a borrowed boat, he entered Jerusalem on a borrowed donkey, he ate the Last Supper in a borrowed Upper Room, and he was buried in a borrowed tomb. Now he asks to borrow the lives of Christians to reach the rest of the world. If we do not speak, then he is dumb and silent.

Third, says Dr. Green, these first Christians were moved to

share their faith out of *a sense of concern.* When he looked at the crowds, Jesus was moved with compassion because they were as sheep without a shepherd. Do we see people as Jesus did? Someone has said that compassion is having "your pain in my heart." Real faith-sharing comes not from compulsion but from compassion. Our motive changes from have-to to want-to when we see people as Jesus did—hungry, lonely, grieving, aimless, and lost.

When Jesus looked at the paralyzed man in Capernaum, he did not say first, "Be healed," but "Be forgiven." Jesus was well aware of this man's physical need. But he was aware, as others were not, of a deeper need—the need of forgiveness, of being put right with God. Because those first Christians accurately diagnosed man's condition as being lost and believed that Jesus was the one answer, they had to share their faith. Canon Green concludes, "If you believe that outside of Christ there is no hope, it is impossible to possess an atom of human love and kindness without being gripped with the great desire to bring men to this one way of salvation."[4]

That first Christian movement was gripped by a great conviction: if man is made for God . . . and if he can be saved or lost eternally . . . then the most important thing in the world is to show men how to be saved.

"Lostness" in an age of tolerance
Today that conviction suffers from tired blood.

Great numbers of Christians are embarrassed to talk about "the soul" or "eternity" or being "lost." Even those of us who subscribe to the ideas expressed in those words don't seem very fired up about them.

For many today, to be "lost" seems to mean that you go to heaven tourist class!

The belief that man is lost is far from the only motive for evangelism. A thousand and one positive reasons exist for winning people to Christ. Yet there is this one great negative: that men *should not perish.* Take that away, and you cut the nerve cord of concern. Trace the history of the movements that have brought great numbers to Christ, and at the heart you will find people who have prayed and witnessed with deeply felt concern.

What has dulled the knife edge of concern today?

For one thing, the general mind-set of our day isn't geared to the idea of dividing into categories of lost and saved. Jesus talked about traveling one of two roads, serving one of two masters, heading toward one of two destinies. We are not comfortable with that either/or kind of talk. We worship at the shrine of the great god Tolerance. The modern mind has shifted into neutral, disliking the pain of distinguishing right from wrong, truth from falsehood. In philosophy, morals, and everyday life, we're told, "Do your own thing." Freedom has come to mean each person is responsible for himself, and no one should try to change another. The revolt against authority has left us with no binding standard. We call this being "liberated," yet fail to recognize the danger of a broad-mindedness that has no moorings.

Because we've become permissive in our own lives, we've also gotten permissive about God. The belief that men are lost doesn't jibe with the idea of God as our "buddy" in heaven. So a new wave of universalism is abroad. Universalism began in the Garden when the serpent told Adam and Eve, "You shall not surely die," and it's often reappeared. Once upon a time universalism told us, "Either men are too good to be damned or God is too good to damn men." The new universalism is more subtle. It admits that men need to be saved, but adds that Christ has already saved them! To oversimplify, historic evangelism has said to men, "Believe on the Lord Jesus Christ, and you'll be saved." The "new evangelism" says to men, "You're already saved. Believe it!" This is a sure way to short-circuit evangelistic urgency. If all men are "doomed to be saved," what's the rush?

Searing social problems also stab our consciences and demand first call on our energies. When we sit with starving babies in our arms, a nuclear bomb over our heads, and pollution poisoning our air, it's very tempting to say, "First, let's change the earth; then we can talk about heaven." On this issue, Christians tend to polarize into two camps: the soul savers and the social reformers. But the core issues are: Can we change the world without saving individuals? And can we really be saved without going on to try to change the world?

Then too, a new sense of honesty and realism has humbled

our self-righteousness. No longer can we think of a missionary as a superior soul from Canada-the-Good or America-the-Beautiful going to set the poor heathen right. The events of the past few years have forced us to face our own shortcomings. We've learned that God is not a great white father and that Jesus doesn't wear red, white, and blue.

If we've candidly examined our own Christian experience, we've had to admit that believing in Jesus hasn't made all our hang-ups disappear. Even though he may have profoundly changed our lives, we still fail and fall. So when someone says, "Jesus is your thing, TM is mine," we may be tempted to ask, "Who am I to tell anyone else what to believe?"

Add to that the fact that not too many people we meet seem overanxious about getting "saved," at least in the traditional sense. Boswell recorded a conversation Samuel Johnson had with Sir Joshua Reynolds about his fear of death. "What are you afraid of?" asked Reynolds.

"Damnation, sir," replied Johnson, "damnation."

Unless I miss my guess, not too many people have said that to you recently! What do you give the man who has everything? How do you relate Jesus Christ to the playboy who couldn't care less? To the friendly Hindu student down the hall? To the agnostic with the social conscience? To the engineer who believes man now has the capability to do anything? How concerned can you be about people who don't feel lost?

Has the age when man needed God now faded into the age of the self-sufficient man who has everything?

Or have we been taken in by the image-makers?

Which is the true-to-life picture—the man of distinction and the God who is dead? Or the man who is alienated and the God who is there?

Let's see how Jesus related in a similar situation to Zacchaeus, the IRS official. Zacchaeus didn't seem to need God. He was a comfortable materialist, a "successful sinner" who had disregarded traditional moral codes and religious customs, and had made it. To most of his contemporaries, Zacchaeus didn't seem very lost.

Then came Jesus, bringing his religious movement to Jerusalem, and on the way passing through Jericho where Zacchaeus lived. A strange thing happened. Driven by longings no one guessed were there, Zacchaeus, the man who had everything, rushed to the main street, tried to elbow his way through the crowd, and finally climbed a tree, trying to see Jesus.

Luke records that when Jesus came by, he looked up at Zacchaeus and called him by name! "Zacchaeus," he said, "quick! Come down! For I am going to be a guest in your home today!"

Zacchaeus quickly climbed down and took Jesus to his house in great excitement and joy. There he said, "Sir, from now on I will give half my wealth to the poor, and if I find I have over-charged anyone on his taxes, I will give him back four times as much!"

And Jesus told him, "Salvation has come to this home today. This man was one of the lost sons of Abraham, and I, the Son of Man, have come to search for and to save the lost."

The key to this encounter is the way Jesus saw Zacchaeus. He didn't view him superficially. He had a deep view of Zacchaeus. He could sense the gap between God and this man, because he was in contact with both!

I believe our sense of human lostness will be in direct propor-tion to the quality of our relationship with God and with others. Evangelistic concern is born when, like Jesus, we walk *with* God *among* people. Break either of those contacts, and we grow cold.

Jesus didn't go out of his way to find Zacchaeus. Jesus was focusing on God's will when he became aware of the need of this man along the way. Doesn't this suggest that Christian witnessing is more a way of life than a program? We sometimes try to be concerned for the millions without Christ, and our emotions won't take it. We're not big enough. Only God can carry the burden of the world. He asks us simply to start with one person we come across.

How did Jesus sense Zacchaeus's need? Had someone told him about Zacchaeus? Had he met him before? Or was it just his divine intuition? I don't know. But I do believe we, as his followers, can discern people's needs *if we're willing to listen*. All around us—in huge, lonely cities, on busy campuses, in affluent homes—people plead, "Won't someone please listen to me!" Are we close enough to hear the "soul English" in their cries?

When I hear people say, "Modern man isn't concerned about salvation," I feel like saying, "Nonsense! Even though people may not talk about damnation, most of what they're saying is about being lost and saved!"

Listen to the songs being written. Joni Mitchell sang, "We are starlight, we are golden, and we've got to get ourselves back to the garden." There, in almost biblical words, is the significance and the lostness of humanity.

Read what the social critics are saying. In *The Making of a Counter-Culture,* Theodore Roszak has given a devastating analysis of our dead-end technocratic society. He closes his introduction with this paragraph:

> I find myself unable to see anything at the end of the road we are following with such self-assured momentum but Samuel Beckett's two sad tramps waiting forever under that wilted tree for their lives to begin. Except that I think the tree isn't going to be real, but a plastic counterfeit. In fact, even the tramps may turn out to be automatons . . . though, of course, there would be great programmed grins on their faces.[5]

Roszak is saying, "Of course, man is lost. Are you too blind to see it? Can't you see that history as we know it has no purpose? That nature has no reality? That man has no significance?"

Even those who deny God can't escape from guilt. Though they don't take it to a clergyman, they do take it to a psychiatrist. Our mental hospitals are half-full of patients with no organic troubles, who suffer from guilt complexes or other stresses. Before this school year is over, one thousand college students will have committed suicide, many because they can't escape their sense of failure.

People who don't see themselves as lost from God will freely admit they have lost the meaning of life. The longing for significance expresses itself most clearly in the fear of death. Neil Simon, who wrote *The Odd Couple* and *Barefoot in the Park,* was asked on the Dick Cavett Show whether making a lot of money concerned him. The studio went dead silent when Simon answered, "No . . . what does concern me is the fear of dying."

How many live with a terrible sense of loneliness, when even in a crowd no one seems real? How many others are gripped by despair about the world situation? One student, asked why he was on drugs, said, "Because I know the wrong finger on the right trigger will end the world, and I live for today because tomorrow may never come."

Underneath the veneer of having everything are many modern people who really do have a deep sense of need, if we wait long enough and probe lovingly to find it.

One time my wife and I were asked to go for a cruise on Long Island Sound on the yacht of a wealthy couple. Our hostess was a well-known figure in show business at one time, and married to one of the top financial men in New York. Jeannie and I were just out of seminary, where we had lived on sixty dollars a week in a one-room apartment without a bathroom, and you can imagine we felt intimidated and very much out of place. We looked at this woman with her servants, her diamonds, her yacht, her many activities, and I thought to myself, *She's got just everything.*

How could we possibly relate Jesus Christ to her? We talked to her about what Christ meant to us, and she listened politely but made it clear she wasn't interested. But as the day went on, a subtle change began to take place. She began to talk about her life—the posing for society, the emptiness, the feeling of being used, of not knowing who her real friends were. She admitted her life was a loveless existence, and in front of the entire group, she finally dissolved into tears.

Get behind the mask, as Jesus did with Zacchaeus, and you find the misery. One of the best ways to do that is to listen with real interest. When you listen with love, it's like putting your hand into the other's life and feeling gently along the rim of his soul until you come to a crack, a frustration or longing that he may or may not be conscious of.

But how deep is that crack? And what will it take to fix it?

The way things really are

There are many who would have looked at Zacchaeus and agreed that he needed a psychological salvation from his hang-ups, or a sociological salvation from his hostilities. But when Jesus looked at him, he saw a man who was lost because he was alienated from God.

From the Christian perspective, all of man's alienations (the word that's so popular in the twentieth century) come because man is under the wrath of God. The first three chapters of Genesis show us that man is significant (made in "the image of God") and yet is sinful, in rebellion against God. Because of the sin, man is expelled from the Garden—alienated from God. Something dies inside man—there's the beginning of psychological alienation. Cain kills Abel—the beginning of sociological alienation. The ground is cursed because of man's fall—the beginning of ecological alienation.

The reality of God's wrath is as much a part of the biblical message as God's grace. "Whoever puts his faith in the Son has eternal life, but whoever rejects the Son will not see that life, for God's wrath remains on him" (John 3: 36). Yet the concept of God's wrath is hard to accept. Why? Perhaps because our own anger is so often selfish and mean. I blow my stack because things don't go my way. I punish my children before I get all the facts because I'm tired.

But God's wrath isn't like mine, just as God's love is different than mine. Where my love is often fickle, God's love is faithful. And where my anger is often petty, God's wrath is pure. Whereas I "fly off the handle," God is "slow to anger" (Exod. 34: 6). God's wrath is his settled, sure hostility to sin. It is not *vindictive;* it is *vindicative.* It is the active, resolute action of God to vindicate justice, uphold the moral law of the universe, and punish sin.

God's blessing is eternal life; his wrath is eternal death. Where sin comes, death follows (Rom. 5: 12). In the Bible, the word *life* means more than physical life, and *death* means more than physical dissolution. Death means we lose something essential to the kind of life we were made for. Life means fellowship with God; death means to lose that fellowship, both now and hereafter in hell.

Does the thought of hell seem to belong to the Dark Ages? If so, Leslie Weatherhead, a well-known liberal thinker, has written that we do our generation a great disservice if we make light of sin and pretend that it does not matter, and that we are all going to the same place, and that God will pat everyone on the head and say, "There, there, it doesn't matter. I'm sure you didn't mean it. Come now and enjoy yourselves." Many things we don't know about hell. But Jesus and the New Testament writers used every image in their power to tell us that hell is real, it's terrible, it's something to be feared, and something to avoid. In his description of the last judgment, Jesus taught that some would go to eternal punishment, some to eternal life (Matt. 25: 46). In other words, hell will be as real and as lasting as heaven.

The horror of hell is not physical pain. After all, the Bible tells us hell was "prepared for the devil and his angels" (Matt. 25: 41), and they're not physical beings. Rather the fire and outer darkness and thirst depict spiritual separation from God, moral remorse, the consciousness that one deserves what he's getting.

Hell is disintegration—the eternal loss of being a real person. In hell the mathematician who lived for his science can't add two and two. The concert pianist who worshiped himself through his art can't play a simple scale. The man who lived for sex goes on in eternal lust, with no body to exploit. The woman who made a god out of fashion has a thousand new dresses but no mirror! Hell is eternal desire—eternally unfulfilled.

But there's another side. G. K. Chesterton once remarked, "Hell is God's great compliment to the reality of human freedom and the dignity of human personality."[6]

Hell, a compliment?

Yes, because God is saying to us, "You are significant. I take you seriously. Choose to reject me—choose hell if you will. I will let you go."

Incidentally, if we really grasp the Bible's view of man— sinful but significant—then we won't get caught in the artificial hang-up between social action and evangelistic concern. Because man is lost but of great value, the two belong together.

If a person doesn't have a soul, then compassion is pointless. Why care for someone if he is only a chance chemical accident? Man is valuable because he's significant. He's significant because he's morally and spiritually responsible. And because he's responsible, he really is lost. That's why our practical concern for earthly welfare must grow out of an overarching concern for eternal destiny.

Love for lost men led God to send his Son.

Love led Jesus to seek and save them at the cost of his life.

If I have bread, and another man is hungry, and I don't share, do I love him?

If I know Christ, and another man is lost, and I don't share, how does the love of God dwell in me?

When I become more concerned with the eternal welfare of another person than what he thinks of me, love has to go into action. We don't evangelize from a superiority complex. We don't go in with an attitude of condemning others. Jesus didn't condemn Zacchaeus. He knew he was lost, but he didn't preach hell to him. He just said, "Zacchaeus, come down; I want to stay at your house." And confronted with Jesus' love, Zacchaeus faced his sin and found salvation. Jesus came to save, not condemn.

Jesus is "the true light that gives light to every man" (John 1:9). All who reject it condemn themselves. They show in running from the light that they prefer evil over true good. But those who come to the light find life.

Doesn't this put evangelism in a different perspective? We don't go to others saying, "You're all wrong, and I've got the answers." We go saying, "I'm in the same boat with you. We've both failed. I identify with you. I can take my mask off and admit my failures and prejudices. But let me point you to Jesus, the light. I'm not what I should be. I'm not what I'm going to be. But because of him, I'm not what I used to be!"

That's witnessing! And we are witnesses, not judges. It's my responsibility to witness. It's God's responsibility to judge.

I suspect Zacchaeus trusted Jesus because he sensed this man was ready to die for him. And I suspect people will believe what we say about Jesus when they see we're willing, in some sense, to die for him and them.

Maybe the world doesn't believe, because it doesn't believe the believers believe.

Some time ago a black brother of mine, a member of the Billy Graham team, came to my room. The night before he'd met until 1:30 with black students at a Pennsylvania school. They were committed to revolution, he told me. They were ready to die for it. Christ, they had told him, was irrelevant and powerless in their situation. And as he told me, he became so burdened that he cried in my arms, a strong man wracked with sobs.

Two days later I got word from the person who arranged that

meeting that my teammate had gotten through to those students as no one ever had. The response was evident the next Sunday when he spoke in that college town and thirty students, black and white, committed their lives to Christ. And then I learned what had gotten through—what had really reached them.

At the end of that late-night session my brother had looked at the students and said, "Okay, you say you're ready to die. Well, I want you to know I'm ready to die too. And you can kill me right here if it will make you feel any better. But I want you to know this. If you die, you die for nothing. If I die, I die for something."

Is man really lost?

Don't answer too glibly.

For if we say yes, then Jesus may say, "Come with me, disciple . . . to Jericho . . . to Jerusalem . . . to Calvary . . . and to the ends of your world."

1.   Leighton Ford, *The Christian Persuader* (New York: Harper & Row, 1966), pp. 11-12.

2.   Michael Green, *Evangelism in the Early Church* (Grand Rapids, Mich.; Eerdmans, 1970), p. 236.

3.   Green, *Evangelism in the Early Church*, p. 245.

4.   Green, *Evangelism in the Early Church*, p. 249.

5.   Theodore Roszak, *The Making of a Counter Culture* (New York: Doubleday, 1969), p. xiv.

6.   G. W. Barrett and J. V. L. Casserly, eds., *Dialogue on Destiny* (Greenwich, Conn.: Seabury, 1955), p. 76.

4

Does the Gospel Really Work?

Lausanne, Switzerland. July, 1974. Nearly four thousand participants from around the world had come to this beautiful city for the International Congress on World Evangelization.

Those of us who served on the planning committee had felt it would be rather ridiculous to meet for ten days to talk about evangelism and not do something to make a public impact for the gospel in Switzerland itself. So on a rather wet Sunday, the local football stadium was the site of a large open-air rally. A huge crowd from Switzerland and nearby parts of France gathered to hear speakers from around the world.

An Indian neurosurgeon of Hindu background told how Jesus Christ had freed him from depression and guilt and had given him joy in serving others.

A Japanese evangelist, raised as a Buddhist, described the brokenness of his boyhood home and the emptiness of his own life until an encounter in high school with a woman missionary led him to Jesus Christ.

An African bishop born in a home centered in tribal religion told how the forgiveness of Jesus Christ had liberated him from the disease of hatred.

Then Billy Graham, a farm boy from the rural southern United States, spoke simply and directly to that sophisticated crowd of contemporary Swiss. He shared the same gospel that Paul shared two thousand years before.

That afternoon, hundreds quietly and simply responded to these simple cross-cultural presentations of Jesus Christ.

Returning to his hotel after the rally, a pastor from Fiji was approached by a young Swiss who wanted to know what had been going on at the stadium that afternoon. When the Fijian pastor told him about Christ, the man invited him home. There the pastor had the privilege of leading this man and his family to Christ. "Imagine," said this citizen of the land of the Reformation, "you came all the way from the South Pacific to share with me a message we have known in this country for many, many centuries."

As I heard that story, I thought to myself once again, "I can be proud of the gospel of Jesus Christ. It is good news. It works powerfully. And it's offered to all people."

I am obligated both to Greeks and non-Greeks, both to the wise and the foolish. That is why I am so eager to preach the gospel also to you who are at Rome. I am not ashamed of the gospel, because it is the power of God for the salvation of everyone who believes: first for the Jew, then for the Gentile. For in the gospel a righteousness from God is revealed, a righteousness that is by faith from first to last, just as it is written: "The righteous will live by faith" (Rom. 1:14-17).

TO PAUL, THE GOSPEL WAS A CAUSE for glory. It was not a theory; it was a truth, a power, tested in the crucible of his own experience, validated in the marketplace of ideas. It was true. It worked. It was for everyone.

Perhaps the root of our modern timidity is right here. If we want to become excited about sharing our faith, we need to get rid of our misconception that the gospel does not work, that people are not interested in Christ, that they won't respond.

What we have to communicate is not merely good advice. It is good news! That's the literal meaning of the word *gospel.*

Originally the Greeks had used it to describe the reward given to a messenger who brought good tidings. Later it came to mean the good news itself. A slave who came with news of a general's victory was said to be "gospeling." One of the Roman emperor Augustus's publicity flacks puffed his birthday as "the beginning of the gospel for the world"! But it is only in the New Testament, where it appears some seventy times, that *gospel* carries the tremendous meaning of good news for all people.

The gospel is described in so many varied and different ways in the New Testament that it's almost impossible for us to grasp its many-sided significance. It is the good news of hope (Col. 1: 23), peace (Eph. 6: 15), reconciliation (Eph. 3: 6), life and immortality (2 Tim. 1: 10), and salvation (Eph. 1: 13), based on the risen Christ (2 Tim. 2: 8). This is a word that speaks to people of every condition—those who are tired of lies, those living in despair, those who are twisted and pulled apart, those who have grown cynical, those afraid of death, those living with a great emptiness inside.

Evangelical Christians have agreed for years that the gospel is summed up in Jesus Christ—who he is and what he has done for our salvation by dying and rising again. But we are also beginning to discover that there are other dimensions of the gospel that we may have overlooked or skipped over too lightly.

According to the New Testament, the gospel is also good news about the Kingdom of God. Mark's Gospel begins with Jesus in Galilee "proclaiming the good news of God. 'The time has come,' he said. 'The kingdom of God is near. Repent and believe the good news!' " (Mark 1: 14, 15). Immediately as he was walking along the shore, he called some fishermen to come and follow him. Jesus' good news was that with his appearance, God's rule had come to a decisive point. Christ didn't implement this Kingdom of God by starting a new political party. Neither did he consign this Kingdom to a far-off future. Instead, he began a new community of disciples who would follow him.

When Jesus preached his first sermon in the synagogue at Nazareth, he highlighted another aspect of the gospel. He unrolled the scroll to the Book of Isaiah and read these words, "The Spirit of the Lord is on me; therefore he has anointed me to preach good news to the poor. He has sent me to proclaim freedom for the prisoners and recovery of sight for the blind, to release the oppressed, to proclaim the year of the Lord's favor." And then he told the people, "Today this scripture is fulfilled in your hearing" (Luke 4: 16-21).

The background of that passage from Isaiah is interesting. Many Bible scholars think it refers to the Year of Jubilee. Every fifty years the Jewish people were supposed to cancel all debts, set all slaves free, and return all land that had been sold (except in the walled cities) to the original owners. So far as we know, this Year of Jubilee had never actually happened. Jesus was really saying to the people, "Today the Year of Jubilee begins!" This gospel was the good news of liberation—setting free of the poor, the prisoners, the blind, and the oppressed.

Paul says that "through the gospel the Gentiles are heirs together with Israel, members together of one body, and sharers together in the promise in Christ Jesus. I became a servant of this gospel by the gift of God's grace" (Eph. 3: 6, 7). Through the gospel, God has broken down the high wall that divided Gentiles and Jews, and he has created one new people.

When he wrote to the Corinthians, Paul told them that "we do not preach ourselves, but Jesus Christ as Lord" (2 Cor. 4: 5). Here he includes the lordship of Jesus Christ in the gospel.

We could put together many other passages. But these few serve to show that *gospel* is a much richer and fuller term than we often realize. The gospel is the good news that, through the death and resurrection of Jesus Christ, God has made available forgiveness of sins and the power of the Holy Spirit to become new persons—living in a new Kingdom, experiencing a new liberation, being part of a new people, and serving a new Lord. There is a sweeping vastness to this gospel that almost takes our breath away.

It is important to realize that this gospel is not a command, but an announcement! The gospel is not an imperative "do," but an indicative "done!" God has done for us in Jesus Christ something we could never do for ourselves.

Good news vs. bad news

Our modern understanding of the gospel is often not quite so dynamic. In fact, I believe that a major reason for our hesitancy to evangelize is our tendency to "plus" Jesus. Somehow we have got the gospel figured out as Jesus plus civic duty, or Jesus plus middle-class values, or Jesus plus the superiority of Western civilization. When we hesitate to load all these things onto people, we are right; we are not sure they want them or need them! As one searching young man asked, "Why do I need religion? I've got a mother who preaches at me, a dad who lays down the law, a sister who is trying to reform me, and a kid brother who lifts a weekly collection out of my pockets. Why do I need church?"[1]

It is true that, for the gospel to be good news, there has to be some bad news. This is what we discussed in the previous chapter: the fundamental predicament of the human race. As a diamond laid against a dark cloth sparkles in all its brilliance, so against the blackness of man's failure the greatness of God's rescue stands out in startling contrast.

Our problem is often in communicating the good in the good news. Many times we have made it seem as if the gospel itself were bad news. Perhaps that's one reason many people don't go to church anymore—they always left feeling more condemned than when they came.

I picture it this way: a rock climber has almost reached the top of the cliff, when suddenly he loses his footing and begins to fall. He quickly grabs a little root that is sticking out of the cliff, holds on for dear life, and yells, "Help!"

That is the insecurity of modern man—holding onto gods that are too small, feeling himself slipping into the abyss below.

Now suppose we look over the cliff and see him. What do we say? Here are some possible options:

- "Sir, I notice you are slipping; please think of the possibilities in your situation and try to hold on more firmly."
- "If you'll try to hold on with one hand, I'll give you a copy of the Ten Commandments of Rock Climbing in the other so you won't fall again."
- "When you get tired of hanging there, would you like to attend our church Sunday?"
- "Pardon me, but would you care to contribute to charity?"

● "Have you compared your situation with that African (or that Indian) hanging over there? I really think your American root is much superior to the Asian or African variety."

Which of these options is good news for the climber?

The only good news would be for you to reach down, grasp his wrist, and pull him up.

Jesus Christ is pictured in Scripture as the strong right hand of God, intervening in our human predicament, reaching down to rescue us and lift us from our lostness. This is not a message that changes from age to age. It is something that happened once in history and is good news for all time.

Good newscasting

In communicating our faith, the challenge is to combine a sense of the absolute truth and urgency of this good news with a sense of the dignity and significance of other people. If this gospel is true, we have an obligation to share it. We have no right to hold it to ourselves. But neither do we have any right to force anyone else to respond.

Almost all of us know people with an attitude of "My way is the only way, and if you don't see it my way, there's something wrong with you." Sensitive people react against a proselytizing based on this prejudice. In reaction, many Christians decide, "My faith is a personal matter. I don't witness because I have no right to intrude upon the privacy of someone else." This tension between our convictions and our respect for the rights of others can be a real hang-up.

Recently I was asked to speak at a national dialogue of Jewish and evangelical Christian leaders. It was interesting that they had invited me, a Christian evangelist. However, I didn't assume they expected me to give a gospel invitation. Neither did I want merely to mouth platitudes about brotherhood. The dilemma of what to say really concerned me, and I thought long and prayed hard about it.

Finally, I asked a local rabbi out for lunch. I asked him what approach he thought I should take. He suggested that the important thing was to share myself, to reveal my personal convictions and feelings without reservation.

Taking his advice, I decided that my presentation at this dialogue would be in the form of an open letter to my rabbi friend. In it I told him why I was a Christian and why I was an evangelist. I explained that I would not be telling the truth unless I affirmed that my Christian faith compelled me to share it with all people—Jesus our Lord told us to go into all the world and preach the gospel to all nations. I wanted him (and all people) to believe that Jesus Christ was the Messiah. I really did.

But while preparing for this dialogue, I had read a lot of history about relationships between Christians and Jews. I knew that the Christian track record had been pretty bad. It was painful to read how so-called Christians had tried to convert Jews in ways that completely denied the spirit of Christ. Sometimes Jews had been forced by law to go to church and hear sermons designed to convert them. For generations in some countries, Jews had been made to stand in front of churches on Good Friday and be slapped on both cheeks as a reprisal for what Jesus had undergone.

In my letter, and to the Jewish participants in the dialogue, I repudiated that kind of spirit and tried to explain the difference between cultural Christians and those who have really been born again and share the spirit of Jesus. Although I wanted them to understand and believe in Jesus as the Messiah, I was not going to coerce or manipulate. And whether or not they accepted Christ, I wanted to honor them as a people, develop friendships with them, and share in many common concerns.

The response to this kind of presentation was largely positive. Most of the participants appreciated my not holding back my desire for them to believe in Jesus, and at the same time extending to them an unconditional friendship.

Not everything that goes under the name of evangelism can get our stamp of approval. Some presentations of the *good news* are anything but. People have been offered "freedom" in the name of Christ in a way that almost denies their freedom. The way we share our faith has to be judged by what the Bible teaches concerning the nature of God, the nature of man, and the nature of the gospel. If I try to get people into the Kingdom of God by arm-twisting and brainwashing, then I am repudiating the love of God. His love is relentless but never coercing. I am also denying what the Bible tells me about the nature of man. Man is made with responsible freedom—allowed by God even to deny him.

But while we disavow the kind of witnessing that smacks of bigotry, we shouldn't fall into the opposite trap of thinking all tolerance is good. I don't tolerate my children eating poison. A lot of what goes by the name of tolerance is merely a lack of convictions. Tolerance is only meaningful if a person believes something very strongly and yet respects the right of others to disagree.

The early Christians had a rocklike conviction that the gospel was the power of God to salvation. "There is no other name under heaven given to men by which we must be saved," they asserted (Acts 4: 12). That's pretty tough faith. Yet, they would not force or bribe anybody to believe. Rather than taking up a sword, they themselves went to death.

Robert Speer, a great missionary leader in the early part of this century, used to say, "You say you have a faith? Well, then either give it out or give it up." Faith is personal, but never private.

Most honest people will respect us if we tell them what we really believe about Jesus Christ, provided we share our faith with humility and modesty, and that they understand we sincerely believe we have received some good news that we have no right to keep to ourselves.

More than just a message

A second important conviction is that the gospel is power and not mere words or ideas. "I am not ashamed of the gospel," wrote Paul, "because it is the power of God." It is not a theory or a theology about power; it is power. *Dunamis* is the word he uses—the root from which we get our word *dynamite*.

Recently a young man told me how he became a Christian while at Arizona State University. As a student of political science, he had become disillusioned with the system, a cynic afraid to believe too much in anything. Then a girl asked him to go to a weekend conference, where he got into a deep discussion about Christianity with the main speaker. "Look," he said, "I'm so fed up that if you gave me the little red button that would send off the missiles and start a nuclear war, I'd push it!"

But to his chagrin, the man thoughtfully replied, "Well, you know you can't do it. So what are you going to do?"

Sobered by that question, he realized he had no alternative.

And that led him to investigate the gospel and eventually to discover for himself that "it *is* the power of God for salvation."

I sometimes think that the very word *salvation* needs to be saved—redeemed from misunderstanding. Use the word *saved* with some people, and they will respond either with a grin of embarrassment or a blank stare because they don't understand what you are talking about.

Part of the problem is that Christians don't always understand what the Bible means when it talks about salvation. Some Christians have too narrow a definition. To them, being saved means simply the initial experience of accepting Christ. Often they think of this as a one-time, highly charged emotional experience.

Among other modern Christians, it has become popular to broaden the word until it loses its sharpness. Salvation becomes social and political liberation.

In the Bible, salvation has the idea of a rescue operation. It's a picture word. It conveys being let out of a cramped, narrow place into broad openness. It has the feeling of running on a beach or through a field with the wind blowing through your hair. It is a power-packed concept that may be expressed by the modern word *liberation*. But what kind of liberation are we talking about?

Salvation is more than a single tense! It is not enough just to say, "I have been saved." If you are going to be true to the New Testament, you have to say, "I have been saved, I am being saved, I shall be saved." Salvation means not just being set free *from* something but also being set free *for* something.

If we really want to describe salvation, we have to put it something like this:

- *Salvation in the past tense:* "I *have been* saved *from* the judgment, condemnation, and guilt of my sin *for* the experience of being a child of God."
- *Salvation in the present tense:* "I *am being* saved *from* self-centeredness *for* the service of God and others."
- *Salvation in the future tense:* "I *shall be* saved *from* wrath and the decay that sin causes *for* the total remaking of our personalities, our bodies, and the whole creation."

As British preacher John Stott emphasizes:

In each phase of personal salvation scripture lays its emphasis not on our rescue (from wrath, from self, from decay and death) so much as on the freedom which this rescue would bring—freedom to live with God as our Father, freedom to give ourselves to the service of others, and finally the "freedom of glory" and to get rid of all the limitations of our flesh and blood existence, until we are free to devote ourselves without reserve to God and to each other![2]

The power by which God frees us from sin, self-centeredness, and death is, paradoxically, the weakness of the cross. God identified himself with us in our lostness, humbling himself to a criminal's death on the cross, dying for our alienation that he might live in us by resurrection power! "The message of the cross is foolishness to those who are perishing, but to us who are being saved it is the power of God" (1 Cor. 1:18).

If we are embarrassed about Jesus, maybe it is because we are not really convinced about this "power of God." That may be because we need an updated experience with Jesus Christ. If Jesus Christ to me is ancient history, not a current event, then there will be little authentic reality when I try to share him.

David Augsburger has suggested that Jesus today might tell us, "The Kingdom of God is like electricity." If electrical power is going to flow efficiently through a wire, there must be *maximum contact* and *minimum resistance*. Am I living in open daily contact with God? Or am I insulated from him and resisting him? If the answer to the first question is no and the answer to the second question is yes, then God's power will be choked off.

But electrical power is also meant to flow into something else. God's power is always power *to*—power to witness, power to serve, power to share. Power is meant not to be hoarded but to flow, to energize. I am convinced that Christians who never express their faith to non-Christians have a sense of unreality, because they don't see this power at work truly changing people. They keep talking and hearing about "gospel," "salvation," "power," but they never see it work. So they are finally convinced it's just an idea.

For absurdity's sake, suppose that in our churches we worshiped motors. Every Sunday we go to a building where, on a raised platform, sits a motor. It isn't connected to anything—it just sits there. We go and listen to someone lecture about how the motor works. Then we sing hymns about how great the motor is. We stand up and solemnly say, "I believe in the motor." We even have people stand up once in a while and tell how ten years ago they were introduced to the motor and ever since they have had safety, security, and happiness. Every Sunday someone exhorts us to believe more in the motor and tell more people about it. And all the time the motor sits there in the center of the building and does nothing.

After a while, don't you think a terrible pall of unreality would fall on the place? Don't you think that we—and our children—would begin to wonder what was so great about that motor? Don't you think we would begin to wonder whether we were just hypnotizing ourselves into believing in the motor?

Sometimes I have had that experience in my own Christian life. I get to the place where Jesus Christ begins to seem like just words to me. Usually these unreal periods are due to one of two things. Either I have choked up my own contact with Christ, or I have stopped sharing Christ with others. When I get involved in sharing Christ and begin to see others come alive and change, I know that he is not just words. The gospel of Jesus Christ is living power.

Coping with power failure

There is another problem, however, that many of us face. Someone professes to receive Christ, and nothing happens. Or they seem to be changed for a while, and then they fall away.

Recently a TV situation comedy, *One Day at a Time,* had such a story line. A teenage girl found Christ and joined the LOGS, the "Lamb of God" movement. The rest of her family, nominal churchgoers, just couldn't understand her new enthusiasm. One day she told her mother she was going to bring her "Christian project" home. The project turned out to be a drunk she had picked up on skid row. Her mother was horrified but finally agreed to let him stay for a couple of days.

At first the derelict seemed to have been changed. He cleaned up; the girl bought him a new suit, and he sat reading his Bible. But it became obvious to the audience, though not to the naive young believer, that this guy was really using her. She refused to believe her sister's warnings that he was just putting on an act.

Then one day, when everybody was out of the house, he made off with all the liquor, the silverware, the toaster, and the radio. The girl was crushed. But after he'd been arrested, he called her from the police station and admitted he'd stolen the things. He asked her to help.

She rushed off once again as a good Samaritan. At the jail, this angle shooter put on a penitent act. He asked her to say that he hadn't stolen these things, that they'd been given to him, so the police would let him go. She indignantly refused. Then he blew up, swore at her, and told her she was a pious bunch of nothing and to please get out of his life.

Stunned and heartbroken, she raged back that he was nothing but a drunken bum and never deserved her love in the first place. The experience left her shattered, but it also brought her out of her make-believe land into the real world. Her mother concluded the whole experience by saying, "Maybe you just didn't have enough faith in your faith."

If you ever try to share your faith regularly, you are guaranteed to come up to an experience like this. But if you give up every time someone uses you, or the gospel doesn't seem to work, then you will never learn the joy of seeing what the gospel can do.

Why does it not work sometimes?

One cause is that some people don't really believe. Once Jesus could not do mighty works in Nazareth "because of their lack of faith" (Matt. 13:58). Some people can fake a good conversion if they think they are going to get something out of it.

Another reason it sometimes doesn't work is that the person will not deal either with the sin question or with the lordship of Christ. There are people who have "prayed to receive Christ" or "made a decision for Christ" but have never truly repented. When difficult times come and they don't find life any easier, they fall away. They have never recognized their utter self-centeredness and their need to surrender their lives to the lordship of Christ. They have tried to have the benefits of Christianity while maintaining the kingdom of self. It doesn't work.

In still other cases, we expect too much too soon. Real faith is prepared for an overnight miracle but also recognizes that sometimes God's work takes place over a long period of time.

Genuine faith keeps on believing, keeps on loving, keeps on hoping. This is not a question of having "faith in faith" but having faith in God. Not every conversion shows up instantly. Especially those persons with deep personality problems and twisted family situations require patient work, prayer, and love over months and even years before you can begin seeing them emerge into the freedom of Christ.

One man I know accepted Christ, and his life changed radically overnight. For several years he was a glowing witness for Christ. Suddenly, the bottom dropped out. He returned to his former life. His family and friends were deeply disappointed, and their non-Christian acquaintances ridiculed his professed conversion. But after seven years, I saw that man come back into the fellowship of the Lord again and begin to recapture the vitality of commitment.

Another friend of mine, a young pastor, was used to lead a hardened criminal to Christ in a county jail. This man told him, "Now preacher, don't get the big head because I have accepted Christ. You are just the twenty-fifth man."

"What do you mean, I'm the twenty-fifth man?" my friend asked.

"Well," he said, "I can think of at least twenty-four others who have witnessed to me about Christ. And it was the effect of all this together that finally led me to Christ. You just happened to be the twenty-fifth."

Sometimes God works quickly, immediately. Sometimes slowly, patiently. Sometimes we may be the first person, sometimes the fifth, sometimes the twenty-fifth in the process. Not everyone with whom we share Christ will respond. Not all of those who respond will do so sincerely. Not all of those whom we think are sincere will last. Some will go up and down. But as we have patient faith in the power of the gospel, as we continue patiently to share, we will see enough lives transformed to see that the gospel really does have power.

Unloading cultural freight

A final operative conviction that we need about the gospel is that it is not for a favored few but for *all* who respond. As Paul says, it is God's power to save "everyone who believes: first for the Jew, then for the Gentile."

A woman who was attending my wife's Bible class said rather defensively one day, "You know, I am really not religious." One thing we need to overcome is that the gospel is just for "religious" people or middle-class people dressed up in their Sunday clothes. The message is that "*all* have sinned" (Rom. 3: 23) and that "*everyone* who calls on the name of the Lord will be saved" (Rom. 10: 13).

Consciously or unconsciously, many of us have identified the gospel with our culture or with certain cultures with which we are familiar. We sometimes hesitate to witness because we think we are asking people to adopt our particular culture or life-style. What we need to do is ask them to trust and follow Jesus within their own cultural mold. But we get in our minds the picture that Christians ought to look a certain way, and it's hard to strip the cultural imagery off the picture of Jesus.

During the 1960s when beards and long hair first became widespread among young people, I was speaking to a meeting in Lansing, Michigan. When I looked out in the crowd and saw some long-haired young people, my reflex thought was, *Uh-oh, got some radicals out there. I wonder what they're thinking.* I kept glancing at them to see their reaction. Every once in a while I would think, *They're looking pretty skeptical.*

Afterwards, I was stunned when they came up and said, "Praise the Lord, brother! We love Jesus too!" Long hair was not really a hang-up with me. I knew that you couldn't identify Christians by whether they were bristle hairs or mop hairs. But the cultural overhang in my emotions was still there. My cultural instincts had overpowered my theological understanding!

In the days of the early Christians, there was a very crucial cultural issue: could Gentiles become Christians without becoming Jews? Some Jewish Christians were insisting that Gentiles not only had to believe in Jesus but also had to be circumcised. The early Christians called a major council (see Acts 15) and determined that a Gentile did *not* have to become a Jew in order to become a Christian. No circumcision was necessary, only belief in Christ as Savior and a life of trust in him.

Even after the church at Jerusalem accepted the idea that the gospel was intended for Gentiles, their expectation that they would culturally become Jews remained strong. The official position of the church was that converts could keep their own distinctive cultures, but minority resistance to this position continued for some time.

Today the issue is reversed. Many Jews have the impression that they can't become Christians without first becoming, at least culturally, Gentiles. In the last several years, however, significant numbers of Jews have been turning to Christ while retaining their Jewish identity and culture. They call themselves Messianic Jews, have fellowships that worship Christ in Jewish ways, call Communion "the Lord's Seder" rather than "the Lord's Supper." The same reality of the gospel is there but in a different cultural expression.

Faith in Jesus Christ, not cultural uniformity, is the basis of salvation. If we are going to be effective in sharing our faith, we have to learn first to accept other cultures. Then we need to recognize that all cultures have good aspects, but all are also judged by God as failures. Our own culture is no more Christian than many others. As we continue growing, we should humbly recognize that the one Body of Christ may contain many different cultures, and that this diversity can be positive and enriching. As a white Christian, I can learn much about Jesus Christ from the way my black brothers and sisters perceive him from their situation. As a conservative Presbyterian, I can learn a lot about freedom in the Spirit from my Pentecostal brothers and sisters. As a Christian who has grown up in affluent North America, where Christianity has been a part of the establishment, I can learn from my brothers and sisters in Africa, Asia, and Latin America, who have been a persecuted and suffering minority for whom the cross and the lordship of Christ stand out with a sharpness that is often blurred in the so-called Christian West.

If we are calling people to ourselves, our life-style, and our culture, maybe we need to be hesitant. But if we are joyfully inviting our friends and neighbors at home and around the world to trust and follow the Jesus who is Lord of all cultures and captive of none, then we can witness with the same strong conviction that Paul had—"I am proud of the gospel!"

1. David Augsburger, *Witness is Withness* (Chicago: Moody, 1971), p. 74.
2. John R. W. Stott, *Christian Mission in the Modern World* (Downers Grove, Ill.: InterVarsity, 1975), p. 108.

5

Oh Where, Oh Where Is Stan Smith?

The first half of 1975 was one of the hardest times in my ministry. I had been a part of the Billy Graham team for twenty years. I had spoken to millions of people all over the world in every kind of situation. I was a "veteran" in evangelistic work. But during the spring of that year, I began to go through a time of tremendous weakness. Almost every time I stood up to speak, it was with a great sense of fear and anxiety. My self-confidence was virtually gone.

It wasn't that I had any doubts about the truth of what I was preaching. In fact, I knew that people's lives were being touched. Yet I had the strangest feeling that nothing I said was going to be of interest or relevance.

As I prayed and tried to prepare for my messages, the ideas, concepts, and words that came seemed empty and lifeless. I just couldn't imagine getting up and speaking. Every time I did, it was with a sense of foreboding.

I shared these feelings with a few close friends, members of my team, and my wife. They all tried to help; but still I lived in that sense of defeat.

One day I had to speak at a university. It was going to be an open-air meeting, and I was almost paralyzed at the thought. Talking to university stu-

dents has always made me a bit nervous, because I know it's usually a critical audience. On this day I didn't feel as if I could face them.

That morning I was on my knees reading the Bible when the following Scripture came to me, "I am thy shield and thy exceeding great reward" (Gen. 15:1, KJV). These were truly words from God. In my state of mind, I felt so defenseless and vulnerable . . . yet God was saying to me, "Go on out there and speak for me. Don't be afraid of the way people look at you; don't be afraid if they are critical, or if there are jeers or catcalls or sneers or questions that you can't handle. I am your shield; I am your protection and security."

A new insight came into my own identity that morning. Since I was sixteen years old I had been preaching; for years my self-image had been tied to my ability as a public speaker. If that was taken from me, what was left?

But the Lord was saying, "I am thy exceeding great reward." It was just the word I needed. I mattered to God not just because I was a speaker. He simply loved me because he had made me for himself. He himself was my "exceeding great reward."

I spoke that day, though I was still shaky, and I sensed the Lord speaking through me. Through the next weeks the anxiety I had been feeling slowly passed. In a deeper dimension than ever before, I learned that my confidence was not to be in myself and my gift, but in God.

We do not want you to be uninformed, brothers, about the hardships we suffered in the province of Asia. We were under great pressure, far beyond our ability to endure, so that we despaired even of life. Indeed, in our hearts we felt the sentence of death. But this happened that we might not rely on ourselves but on God, who raises the dead (2 Cor. 1:8, 9).

TENNIS IS MY GAME. I'm not a great player, just a middling-to-average one, but I enjoy playing. Once or twice a year the pros usually come to Charlotte, my hometown, on their annual tour. If I'm in town, I try to see several matches. After watching the pros a couple of times, a peculiar thing happened to my own game: it seemed to fall apart!

I would watch Stan Smith or Arthur Ashe or Jimmy Connors and then say to myself, "Now I know how to do it, and I'm going back and blow my opponents off the court." Back on my home court, my mind would bark out instructions to my body as I prepared to serve.

"Okay, now get your feet in a forty-five degree angle behind that line. Toss that ball up just to the right position. Bring your racket behind. Smash it into that serve. Bring your back foot forward, and turn your body into it. Blaze an ace in there!"

And my body would reply, "Who, me?" as that great "ace" thunked into the net!

I found that watching the pros actually hurt my game. When I realized I couldn't do it like Stan Smith, that I was still playing like Leighton Ford, I would get frustrated and almost want to quit.

Something similar often happens to us Christians. We go to a meeting or a conference. We hear a Billy Graham preach a powerful message, a Corrie ten Boom testify how God has led her, a Josh McDowell give a brilliant presentation on how to answer skeptics' questions. Or we listen to an Ann Kiemel tell how she walks up to complete strangers and starts talking about the love of Christ and how positively they respond.

We say to ourselves, "That's great. I'm ready to go out there and share Christ." But before long, we discover we are still the same person. We are either afraid to share our faith, or if we try, we fall flat on our faces.

Sometimes the fear of others holds us back from sharing our faith. Perhaps as often, it's the fear of ourselves, that sense of personal inadequacy. "I just don't know what to say if I talk to someone else." "What would I share? Christ just doesn't seem real to me." "I am afraid I might mess up and really turn somebody off." "I guess I'm just not the salesman type."

Perhaps the underlying problem is that we have never grasped accurately what the Bible teaches about our self-perception as Christians. We have been taught that pride is wrong and humility is good. But many of us have never learned the difference between pride and a right sense of self-acceptance, nor the difference between humility and self-hatred. We have been taught not to puff ourselves up, so we think that the answer is to put ourselves down. Somehow we have the idea that Jesus' statement about denying ourselves means we are to hate ourselves. Humility is defined as a kind of feeling of worthlessness.

But stop to think: What merit is there in denying myself if I'm not worth anything anyway?

In the biblical view, self-acceptance is not equated with selfishness. There is *good* self-love and *bad* self-love. Good self-love recognizes my value, a person made by God with significance and worth. Genesis tells us that when God finished making man in his own image, "it was very good" (Gen. 1: 31).

But there is also a self-love that is wrong. This comes when we worship ourselves and put ourselves in the place of God. I like to spell sin "s-capital I-n." Here was the essence of temptation that first came to man; the serpent said to Adam and Eve, "You will be like God" (Gen 3: 5, GNB).

Humanity in the biblical view is both significant and sinful. Part of becoming a Christian is having a realistic view of myself, a creature limited but good, made by God, but also a rebel who needs to confess, "God, be merciful to me, a sinner."

When we receive Christ into our lives and he takes up residence there, he cleanses the old cancerous selfishness and hands back our new selves, healed and beautiful!

Counselor Walter Trobisch describes a vicious cycle that most of us have gone through:

"We are unable to love others because we have not learned to love ourselves.

"We cannot learn to love ourselves because we are not loved by others or are unable to accept their love.

"We are not loved by others because we are unable to love them or we love them 'out of duty.'

"We are unable to love them because we have not learned to love ourselves."[1]

Into this vicious cycle comes the dynamic of the good news. Through Jesus Christ, God loves me in spite of what I am. In fact, we are urged in Romans 12 "to offer yourselves as living sacrifices, holy and *pleasing to God*—which is your spiritual worship" (vs. 1). Imagine—sinful human beings such as you and I, redeemed and cleansed by Christ—able to offer ourselves to him as valuable and pleasing!

But this is more than a theological truth. God's acceptance has to grip us in the very center of our personality.

One night our young son Kevin was praying. He thanked God for his mother and father and brother and sister, and then he closed by saying, "God, thank you for even me!"

Have you ever said that to God? "Thank you for my gifts and for my limitations. Thank you for my family, even with all its problems. Thank you for my looks, my personality, the situation I'm living in, all the experiences I have gone through, the good and the bad." Have you ever realized that God has made you the special person you are so you can uniquely relate to him and uniquely relate Jesus Christ to others?

"God loves me so much he will accept me just as I am, but he loves me too much to leave me that way."

I don't know who coined that phrase, but it gives us the clue for dealing with the inadequacies that hamper us in sharing our faith. All of us have gifts and strong points. All of us have handicaps and limitations. Some of our handicaps come because God allowed us to be born that way. Some are the result of our own sin and selfishness. God's unconditional love frees us to learn both to accept ourselves as God has made us and to change ourselves where we can, with his help.

Joni Eareckson is a beautiful young woman who happens to be a quadraplegic; she lost the use of both arms and both legs in a diving accident when she was seventeen. Four years before, she had come to know Jesus Christ in a personal way as her Savior and Lord. Following the accident, she had a period of tremendous depression. But God brought her through it. She has learned to write and to draw beautifully with a pen held in her mouth.

When I saw her on television, she drew a picture while talking the whole time. Quickly she sketched some houses and trees and then drew a frame around the whole thing. She said, "The frame limits the picture, just as our handicaps limit us. But the frame is not there to draw attention to itself. The frame helps us focus on the area of creativity, the picture. And our handicaps, as we accept them, help us focus on the areas of creativity God has built into our lives."

Just ordinary people

Sometimes we tend to romanticize the early Christians as being a breed of super-heroes with no weaknesses like ours. But that's far from the case.

After Jesus' death, many of his disciples who had run away when he was arrested gave themselves over to complete discouragement. John's Gospel portrays them gathered together in a room locked for fear of their enemies. They were haunted by memories of their failure, intimidated by the menace of a hostile society. Jesus came, stood among them and said, "Peace be with you!" He showed them his hands and side and proved, to their overwhelming joy, that he actually was alive from the dead. "As the Father has sent me, I am sending you," he said. "Receive the Holy Spirit" (John 20: 21-23).

Consider the contrast just a few weeks later. Peter and John announce healing to a crippled man at the Temple. The next day the rulers call them in and begin to question by what power or name they have done this. Peter, filled with the Holy Spirit, boldly testifies that the man was healed by the name of Jesus Christ, whom the rulers had crucified but whom God had raised from the dead. " 'Salvation is found in no one else,' " he says, " 'for there is no other name under heaven given to men by which we must be saved.'

"When they saw the courage of Peter and John and realized that they were unschooled, ordinary men, they were astonished and they took note that these men had been with Jesus" (Acts 4: 12, 13).

This spirit of courage characterizes those first Christians throughout the Book of Acts. When the believers faced opposition, they had a prayer meeting, and "after they prayed, the place where they were meeting was shaken. And they were all filled with the Holy Spirit and spoke the word of God boldly" (4: 31). After Saul encountered the risen Lord Jesus on the way to Damascus, he "preached fearlessly in the name of Jesus" (9: 27). In Antioch, when opponents began to hurl abuse at the missionaries, "Paul and Barnabas answered them boldly: 'We had to speak the word of God to you first. Since you reject it and do not consider yourselves worthy of eternal life, we now turn to the Gentiles' " (Acts 13:46). The same two spent time in Iconium "speaking boldly for the Lord, who confirmed the message of his grace by enabling them to do miraculous signs and wonders" (Acts 14:3).

These examples from Acts help us understand the quality of boldness. It is not rudeness. Nor is it merely the natural characteristic of the extrovert.

Boldness is God-given courage and confidence under pressure that overcomes fear and reserve and produces freedom in speaking the gospel.

It is produced by:

- personal contact with Jesus (4:13; 9:27)
- prayer (4:31)
- being filled with the Holy Spirit (4:31)
- knowledge of and confidence in the Word of God (13:46, 47)
- the sign of God's power at work (14:3)

We have the same handicaps those first Christians had, but we also have the same helper. "The Spirit helps us in our weakness" (Rom. 8:26).

Our family has had the privilege of getting to know Stan Smith and Roscoe Tanner, two of the top tennis pros, and having them visit in our home. It's been an inspiration to see the Christian commitment of these two young men and their desire to grow in the Lord. More selfishly, I've often wished that either of them had time to come to my tennis club. If they could just coach me for a month . . . they could help me change my stance a bit one day. They could help me alter my grip the next. Then they could work on my timing, my positioning, my follow-through. . . .

Unfortunately, Stan Smith and Roscoe Tanner aren't available to be my coaches. But Jesus Christ is! He has done far more than put on an exhibition. He has promised the help of his Spirit, his personal representative. Before Jesus left to go back to heaven, he promised, "I will ask the Father, and he will give you another Counselor, the Spirit of truth, to be with you forever . . . I will not leave you as orphans; I will come to you" (John 14:16-18).

As we share our faith, you and I are not alone. God wants to use us just as we are—providing we are willing for him to make us all he wants us to be!

How does this principle apply to the different inadequacies we mentioned earlier?

"I can't talk to anyone else about Christ because God just doesn't seem real to me."

This is a genuine obstacle. Sharing Jesus Christ is not basically talking about a moral code, our church, or Christian philosophy. It is introducing people to a person. And we can't introduce someone we ourselves have never met.

Timothy, Paul's young protege, was apparently very timid. Paul shared with him the secret of his own confidence: "I am not ashamed, because *I know whom I have believed,* and am convinced that he is able to guard what I have entrusted to him for that day" (2 Tim. 1: 7, 8, 12, italics added).

Witnessing is taking a good look at Jesus and telling what we have seen. The better I know him, the less ashamed I am.

The Holy Spirit enables us to know Jesus Christ, to have the same relationship to him the first disciples had. The Holy Spirit has been called "the applied edge of redemption"; he takes what Jesus Christ did for us twenty centuries ago and applies it to the reality of our lives today.

Some people have only a kind of environmental faith. They have "oozed" into Christianity, having been brought up to know about Jesus and the Bible, but they've never personally entered into a relationship with him. Just as you can study about marriage without being married, so you can study all about Christianity without being a Christian. Christianity, like marriage, is a relationship. The first step to reality may be to put this book down right now and say, "Jesus Christ, I ask you to come into my life. Move in as a living person. Take over the center of my life."

Others have truly been born again, but seem unassured of their relationship to God. A primary ministry of the Holy Spirit is to create this kind of assurance. As Paul wrote, "You did not receive a spirit that makes you a slave again to fear, but . . . the Spirit who makes you sons. . . . The Spirit himself testifies with our spirit that we are God's children" (Rom. 8:15, 16).

Ruth Graham, Billy's wife, was brought up in China as the daughter of a medical missionary. From childhood she knew the gospel but failed to grasp that it was personally for her. One day while reading Isaiah, the Holy Spirit led her to personalize the words she was reading. She read Isaiah 53 like this: "He was wounded for *Ruth's* transgressions, he was bruised for *Ruth's* iniquities . . . and with his stripes *Ruth* is healed." The same Holy Spirit who brought Ruth Graham personal assurance can also convince you that you are no longer a stranger to God, nor even his slave, but one chosen to be his son or daughter.

Our effectiveness in sharing Jesus Christ depends not only on an initial experience of salvation and on our assurance but also on a life-long quest, a progressive, ever-deepening knowledge of him. To reflect Christ in the marketplace, we need to be with him in the quiet place. A daily devotional life of Bible reading, prayer, and meditation is not some kind of legalistic regimen but a wonderful opportunity to fellowship with God and learn to know him better.

For those who have never established this quiet time, or who have stopped and find it difficult to resume, here is a plan from Bob Foster's pamphlet, "Seven Minutes with God."

½ minute—prayer for guidance (Psalm 143:8)
4 minutes—reading the Bible (Psalm 119:18)
2½ minutes—prayer
    adoration (1 Chron. 29:11)
    confession (1 John 1:9)
    thanksgiving (Eph. 5:20)
    supplication (Matt. 7:7)

Foster wisely comments, "This is not a fetish, but a guide. Very soon you will discover that it is impossible to spend only seven minutes with the Lord."

Even though the Holy Spirit has been given to help us perceive God's reality day by day, there will still be times when he seems very unreal. When sharing our faith, it is important to be vulnerable at this point.

Psychiatrist John White writes,

Has it never dawned on you that the essence of witness is just plain honesty? You are salt—whether you feel like it or not. You are not told to act like salt but to be what you are. You are a light. God has done a work in your life. Don't try to shine. Let the light that God put there shine out. Now to let your light shine it demands no more than honesty. It demands honesty before unbelievers. In fact such honesty is in itself ninety percent of witnessing. Witnessing is not putting on a Christian front so as to convince prospective customers. Witnessing is being honest, that is, being true to what God has made you in your speech and in your day by day behavior.[2]

Unbelievers know we are not perfect, and if we try to pretend we are, they will smell that dishonesty. What the world is looking for is reality—not perfect people, but imperfect people in whom the grace of God is working.

Another inadequacy is:
"I just don't have the personality for witnessing."
Many of us have stereotyped the effective witness as the natural salesman, the extrovert, the person who "never meets a stranger." If we are not like that, we feel God can't use us.

A few months ago I was introduced to a layman who has been a key mover in a nationally known lay evangelism program in which hundreds of people have learned to share their faith effectively. I was expecting to meet "Mr. Personality." Instead I met a quiet, gentle dentist who was anything but an extrovert. Yet with his love for Christ and other people, he has obviously found a way of witnessing that is natural for him.

God has made each of us special people. Our personalities, backgrounds, and experiences have equipped each of us to touch people whom no one else could touch. God wants to take the special people we are and work in us to produce uniquely the fruit and gifts of the Spirit.

The fruit of the Spirit does *not* necessarily refer to success in soul-winning but rather to reflecting the character of Jesus Christ—qualities such as love, joy, peace, and patience. The Holy Spirit also works to help each of us discover and develop the spiritual gifts we have been given by God. In the next chapter we will talk further about spiritual gifts. The point is, all the qualities of spiritual fruit are to be seen growing and maturing in all Christians. At the same time, each believer is given at least one spiritual gift with which to serve the Body of Christ.

The spiritual fruit and gifts are not produced by our struggling but are the natural outgrowth of our continuing relationship with Jesus Christ day by day.

In the Middle Ages, a very ordinary man named Brother Lawrence, a cook in a monastery, discovered a spiritual secret one day while sitting beneath a tree. For a long time he had been striving to be a Christian. As he looked at the tree, he thought to himself, "In the cold of winter the tree is dry and barren and unfruitful. As spring comes, new life begins to come and buds appear. Then in summer the blossoms and fruit come. That tree is like my life." He realized he could not make himself into a super personality for God to use. He could only trust God, in his own timing, to work through him as he was and shape him into what he should be. He realized that he could not hurry God. From that time on, as Brother Lawrence prepared food and washed dishes in his kitchen, he rested in what he termed "practicing the presence of God."

As we walk with God and learn that he is working in our lives with every circumstance, we will find latent potential that we never dreamed we possessed.

At a California conference I met an apple-cheeked young farmer to whom God had given a tremendous ministry in his own small city. He would go downtown and invite street people and runaways to spend the night at a home he and some friends had bought. There they would give them a free meal, listen to them, show personal interest, and often have the opportunity to share Christ with them. "I never realized I had any ability to relate to people like this," he told me, his face glowing, "until I just went out to do what I knew God was calling me to do."

A third inadequacy is often expressed like this:

"I just don't know enough to talk to anyone else about God."

Here again the same principle applies: God will use us on the basis of the knowledge we have now, provided we are willing for him to teach us all he wants us to know. If we wait to share Christ until we have a Ph.D. in Bible or have researched two or three answers to every conceivable question that might be asked, then we will probably never witness. Even a spiritual "baby" can share what he has experienced.

An example of this is the blind man whose healing by Jesus is recorded in John 9. When some critics tried to stump him with heavy theological questions, the man simply replied, "I do know one thing: I was blind but now I see!" (vs. 25).

He reminds me of my friend, the Christian singer Bev Shea. Asked by a cynic, "How much do you know about God?" Bev replied, "Not very much, but what I do know has changed my life."

On the other hand, God doesn't want us to be content in ignorance, either. Just because God can use us with a minimum of knowledge is no excuse to ignore the scriptural command to grow in grace and the knowledge of Christ.

Essential to this growth is knowledge of the Scriptures. We need to take seriously Paul's teaching that "all scripture is God-breathed and is useful for teaching, rebuking, correcting and training in righteousness, so that the man of God may be thoroughly equipped for every good work" (2 Tim. 3:16, 17). The Bible tells us what we need to *know*—"teaching"; what we need to *give up*—"rebuking"; what we need to *change*—"correcting"; and what we need to *do*—"training in righteousness." The end result is that we might mature in our Christian life and ministry.

Gaining this vital working knowledge of the Scripture is not a short-term project but a lifelong process. It calls for marathon runners, not sprinters. Nevertheless we start right where we are.

I would suggest these three steps, each one an important ingredient in the recipe for mixing the Scriptures into our lives.

1. Hear. Regular and faithful attendance at church and Bible studies where gifted teachers expound the Scripture is essential.

2. Read. A daily devotional reading to find God's marching orders for each day is fundamental. Consistently fifteen minutes a day of thoughtful reading is the best way to start.

3. Study. An hour a week is certainly the minimum we ought to set aside in one block for a systematic study program of the Bible, basic Christian doctrine, and apologetics (understanding the reasons why we believe and learning to answer objections).*

* For daily devotional reading the best helps I know are the daily Bible reading notes available from Scripture Union, 1716 Spruce St., Philadelphia, PA 19103. One of the best basic Bible study courses is the *Discipleship* series, available from the Navigators, Box 1659, Colorado Springs, CO 80901. Bob Foster's leaflet, "Seven Minutes with

God expects us to study until we have a reasonable grasp of the basics of the gospel. But witnessing is far more than programming ourselves with pre-packaged formulas and answers. Rather, it requires an attitude of faith that trusts God to give us the word he wants when we're in natural situations and when we're under pressure.

Another basic inadequacy is the sheer lack of confidence. *"What if I try—and mess up? I may do more harm than good."*

This is often a problem with people who are basically timid and feel themselves failure-prone. But it is more than that. Others, who have no difficulty at all in closing a difficult sale or zestfully take part in such risk exercises as skiing or surfing, freeze up at the thought of sharing their faith with someone else.

Part of the problem may be that we feel compelled to produce results. But evangelism cannot be judged simply by positive responses. God has called us (1) to proclaim and embody the message, and (2) to disciple those who respond. The actual producing of results is in God's hands. "Neither he who plants nor he who waters is anything, but only God, who makes things grow" (1 Cor. 3: 7). What God expects of us is reliability—"It is required that those who have been given a trust must prove faithful" (1 Cor. 4: 2).

Faithfulness does not mean plodding along with an attitude of indifference. We are to long for people to come to Christ, even implore them to be reconciled to God. Paul once said he would wish himself cursed if that would help others to be saved.

Neither does faithfulness imply a lack of expectancy. I have sometimes heard people rationalize a lack of effectiveness in evangelistic work by saying that all God requires is "faithfulness." Jesus' teaching in the parable of the talents, however, indicates that the faithful servant was also the successful one who invested his talent and multiplied it. Our goal in sharing our faith is to see people become disciples. But faithfulness does mean that we recognize results as ultimately belonging to God.

When I first realized this, it brought a real sense of release and

God," is also available from the Navigators. For doctrine and apologetics I highly recommend Paul Little's books, *Know What You Believe* and *Know Why You Believe*, InterVarsity Press, Box F, Downers Grove, IL 60515.

freedom. At one time, when invited to lead an evangelistic outreach effort, I went with the attitude, "These people have put a lot of money and effort into this project, so somebody better get converted!" As a result, I was often anxious and defensive, unable to relate warmly to other people. Then I got it into my head that God was the evangelist and I was a co-worker with him. That took the pressure off. I could relax. And I found that even more people were responding.

Here again the Holy Spirit is our partner. Jesus said, "When the Counselor comes . . . he will testify about me; but you also must testify" (John 15: 26, 27). It's a partnership that can't be separated. When I am conscious that the Holy Spirit is using me in sharing with someone, I do not have the feeling that some alien presence is taking over. Rather, I feel that I am most truly myself, although I am speaking beyond myself. It is not a weird feeling, but a sense of becoming supernaturally natural.

When I am conscious of the fear of failure holding me back, I go through a kind of personal checklist:

1. Does this fear come basically from pride, a fear that I will not live up to my own expectations or to those of others?

2. Do I remember that God has called me first to faithfulness, then to efficiency?

3. Do I trust that the Holy Spirit is working before me, with me, and through me?

4. Do I remember that I am called to be neither more nor less successful than Jesus Christ was?

5. Do I remember that God does his greatest work when I seem to be weakest? Isn't that, after all, the mystery of the cross?

Several years ago I was scheduled to speak to some Royal Australian Air Force trainees at an early-morning session in the city of Wagga Wagga (one of those marvelous Australian names!). The night before, addressing an open-air rally in damp, cold weather, my voice had become husky. The early-morning session was held in a hangar, which has to be one of the most difficult places to speak because the sound bounces around the steel and concrete.

Five hundred men had gathered. As I stood to speak, I was praying that God would give me the right words to say. I knew many of them had never gone to church in their lives nor had ever been exposed to the gospel.

When I stood up, I saw that the microphone was too low. So I pulled it up, without realizing that the cord was caught under the stand at the bottom. There was a bad connection, and as I pulled it up, the cord snapped off. There I was without a microphone, and a voice that was already half gone.

I began to speak, and in less than five minutes my voice was nothing more than a croak. I presented the basics of the gospel and finished as quickly as I could. I invited anybody who wanted to know more to talk to the chaplain, while I made a fast retreat to some place where I didn't have to talk. Completely discouraged, I felt this great opportunity had been lost.

About a week later I saw the chaplain. He came up, face glowing, and reported, "Remember how you asked men to come speak to me? Well, more than twenty-five of them have come, many have accepted Christ, and others have indicated a definite interest." I was flabbergasted. God's power was independent of the quality of my voice!

His strength is made perfect in our weakness. I learned that day that God does not need a scintillating personality, and he certainly does not call us to any kind of manipulation of people to get "results." The words that Paul wrote so long ago took on a fresh meaning for me, "We do not use deception, nor do we distort the word of God. On the contrary, by setting forth the truth plainly we commend ourselves to every man's conscience in the sight of God. . . . For we do not preach ourselves, but Jesus Christ as Lord, and ourselves as your servants for Jesus' sake. . . .

"But we have this treasure in jars of clay to show that this all-surpassing power is from God and not from us" (2 Cor. 4: 2, 5, 7).

1.   Walter Trobisch, *Love Yourself* (Baden-Baden, Germany: Editions Trobisch, 1976), p. 23.
2.   John White, "Witnessing Is Not Brainwashing," *His* 26, no. 9 (June, 1966).

6

Let My People Grow

I was speaking at an open-air crusade in Halifax, Nova Scotia. Billy Graham was to speak the next night and had arrived a day early. He came incognito and sat on the grass at the rear of the crowd. Because he was wearing a hat and dark glasses, no one recognized him.

Directly in front of him sat an elderly gentleman who seemed to be listening intently to my presentation. When I invited people to come forward as an open sign of commitment, Billy decided to do a little personal evangelism. He tapped the man on the shoulder and asked, "Would you like to accept Christ? I'll be glad to walk down with you if you want to."

The old man looked him up and down, thought it over for a moment, and then said, "Naw, I think I'll just wait till the big gun comes tomorrow night."

Billy and I have had several good chuckles over that incident. Unfortunately, it underlines how, in the minds of many people, evangelism is the task of the "big guns," not the "little shots."

IMAGINE THAT WE ARE TV SPORTSCASTERS standing on the sidelines of a football game to give the play-by-play.

Scene No. 1: The team nearest us is standing together, heads bowed in prayer, with the coach in the center. Suddenly they give a great cheer, and the coach trots out onto the field by himself. The players go sit on the bench.

"What's going on?" we ask as we stick a microphone in front of a 240-pound guard. "What's the coach doing out there?"

"Oh, he's going to play today."

"All by himself?"

"Sure, why not? He's had a lot more experience and training than the rest of us. We've got a lot of rookies on this team, and we might make mistakes. Anyway, they pay the coach well. We're all here to cheer and support him—and look at the huge crowd that's come to watch him play!"

Bewildered, we watch as the opposing team kicks off. The coach catches the ball. He valiantly charges upfield, but is buried under eleven opposing tacklers. He's carried off half-conscious. . . .

You think that's ridiculous? But isn't it the picture many of us have of the church? The members expect the minister to do the preaching, praying, witnessing, and visiting because he's paid to do the Lord's work and he's better trained.

But listen to God's Game Plan. According to Ephesians 4:11, 12, Christ has given the church apostles, prophets, evangelists, pastors, and teachers "to prepare God's people for works of service." God gives leaders to the church, not to do all the work, but to help all of God's people do it! Lay people are not there simply to pay pastors and evangelists to do the Lord's work. Rather, pastors, evangelists, and teachers are to equip the so-called lay people to be ministers!

Your pastor is meant to be a kind of playing coach. His main function is to help you as a Christian discover your spiritual gifts, develop them, and use them to build up the Body of Christ.

Happy huddles

Now look at Scene No. 2: The team realizes they've all got to play, so they're on the field in a huddle. They huddle . . . and huddle . . . and huddle. The referee calls a penalty for delaying the game and moves the ball back five yards. Still the team huddles, huddles, and huddles. The referee calls penalty after penalty, until finally the ball is moved all the way back to their own goal line.

"Hey, coach!" shouts the quarterback to the sidelines. "This is the greatest huddle I've ever been in. What a group of guys! We have the best fellowship . . . and some of these guys are amazing students of the play book. Some have memorized over a hundred plays and can analyze them precisely. We learn so much in this huddle!"

"But why don't you get up on the line and play?"

"Why should we? What we want are bigger and better huddles! Besides, we might get hurt. No one ever got hurt in a huddle!"

Your church and mine are in big trouble if they become a "holy huddle," a band of saints gathered Sunday after Sunday, singing, praising, enjoying each other—but never setting out on the line to apply what they learn. The church is supposed to be Christ's *Body*—his hands, his feet, his voice—by which he carries out his plans in the world. God intends that "through the church, the manifold wisdom of God should be made known" (Eph. 3:10).

The church is to be God's light in a dark, corrupt society. The Christian life was never meant to be lived only in church for a couple of hours on Sunday. It's meant to be lived in the public arena—on the firing line at school, the office, and in the neighborhood, seven days a week. Of course, we need worship and training and fellowship with other Christians—a football team needs the huddle. But it's what happens after the huddle that the game is all about.

Which contest is more important?

Here's Scene No. 3: The team breaks out of the huddle. But instead of lining up against the opposing squad, they break into groups of two or three, arguing with each other. Soon they start shoving, and two of them actually get into a fight.

"What's wrong now?" we ask as one of them walks off the field in disgust.

"That bunch of malcontents can't agree on anything," he says. "Those two over there are arguing over the color of the uniforms. A couple of others are quarreling over the right way to kneel in the huddle. Those two guys are arguing because one believes in what he calls 'personal' football, and the other believes in 'social' football. They can't agree whether the individual or the team is more important. Some of the white players say the blacks should go play on their own field, and some of the black guys don't like the band music. A couple are fighting over whether women should be allowed to play. And I'm quitting because I can pass a lot better than that other guy, and they won't let me be the quarterback."

The Game Plan says that Christ "is our peace. . . . His purpose was to create in himself one new man out of the two [Jew and Gentile], thus making peace . . . to reconcile both of them to God through the cross, by which he put to death their hostility" (Eph. 2:14-16). Christians talk a lot about the peace of Christ. Can the world see that peace in our church relationships?

Within the Body of Christ there is plenty of room for diversity of gifts, but underlying that diversity is unity. "Be completely humble and gentle," writes Paul, "be patient, bearing with one another in love. Make every effort to keep the unity of the Spirit through the bond of peace. There is one body and one Spirit . . . one Lord, one faith, one baptism; one God and Father of all . . . " (Eph. 4:2-6).

Isn't it time to show our oneness in truth and love to a watching world?

A different team

So the first half ends. The team drags off to the locker room defeated, demoralized, beaten.

But when the second half begins, we see a different team. Suddenly they're playing together with a new spirit. They huddle, slap each other on the back, and take the line. They're off the ball with split-second timing, there is no hesitation, they know where they're going. Each player carries out his assignment, and soon they score a touchdown, then another, and another. When the game ends, they've won!

Afterwards in the locker room the players are exhausted, cut, and bruised, but happy.

"What happened at halftime to change this team?" we ask the coach.

"We were sitting here beaten," he says, "and suddenly a kind of presence seemed to come over us. I started talking to the players, pointing out my mistakes and theirs, and they started talking. Everyone was honest. Nobody blamed the others. We took a good look at ourselves. Then someone recalled that the Great Coach, the one who invented the game, also wrote the Master Game Plan. Wouldn't it make sense to see what he said?

"We remembered how he literally gave himself to get the game started and to teach that first team everything he knew. So we got out the original Game Plan and read about basics such as each player knowing his place and dedicating himself to it, about pulling together, being willing to sacrifice, knowing the aim of the game, and using the proper equipment he designed.

"Well, we were quiet. It felt as if the Great Coach was with us, as if somehow his Spirit got inside us. Suddenly, we were up! Motivated! Ready to go! We can't take the credit. It goes to him!"

We figure the coach was right. We'd seen a beaten team become a great team. It had to be something beyond themselves.

The Church of Jesus Christ triumphs not because it's a super-church made up of superpeople with a superstrategy, but because it faithfully obeys the Savior, the head of the Church, Jesus Christ the Lord.

The church: God's purpose

Scripture shows that God is concerned about building new persons but also a new community. Because of today's emphasis on rugged individualism, we often miss the fact that the Church stands at the center of God's purpose. Ever since sin divided brother from brother and Cain killed Abel, God's plan has been to gather a new community centered in himself.

This means that the goal of faith-sharing is not just that a few of our friends may become Christians but "that the body of Christ may be built up until we all reach unity in the faith and in the knowledge of the Son of God and become mature, attaining the full measure of perfection found in Christ" (Eph. 4: 12, 13).

But how do you measure whether a church is growing? Attendance, giving, and size of building may be yardsticks. But the church is more than that. It is a body of people who must be both *counted* and *weighed*—weighed in terms of their commitment to Jesus Christ, to his work in the world, and to each other.

Some people deem it "unspiritual" to quote evangelism statistics. If so, they are more "spiritual" than the writer of the

Book of Acts. Significant numerical growth is frequently noted. When a university fellowship group, or a Bible class, or a church doubles or triples, we ought to rejoice that numbers have turned to the Lord.

It's worth noting, however, that in the Book of Acts numbers are used in *celebration,* not *calculation.* There is no indication they set out deliberately to win three thousand on the Day of Pentecost. When numbers are used, they are always coupled with quality measures, indicators of vital life and growth in other dimensions. Notice how quality and quantity are coupled in the same contexts:

QUANTITY GROWTH	*QUALITY GROWTH*
Those who accepted his message were baptized, and about three thousand were added to their number that day. (2:41)	They devoted themselves to the apostles' teaching and to the fellowship, to the breaking of bread and to prayer. (2:42)
And the Lord added to their number daily those who were being saved. (2:47)	They broke bread in their homes and ate together with glad and sincere hearts, praising God. (2:46, 47)
Many who heard the message believed, and the number of men grew to about five thousand. (4:4)	When they saw the courage of Peter and John and realized that they were unschooled, ordinary men, they were astonished and they took note that these men had been with Jesus. (4:13)
More and more men and women believed in the Lord and were added to their number. (5:14)	The apostles performed many miraculous signs and wonders among the people. And all the believers used to meet together. . . . No one else dared join them, even though they were highly regarded by the people. (5:12, 13)

The number of disciples in Jerusalem increased rapidly, and a large number of priests became obedient to the faith. (6: 7)	In those days when the number of disciples was increasing, the Grecian Jews among them complained . . . because their widows were being overlooked in the daily distribution of food. So the Twelve gathered all the disciples together and said . . . "Brothers, choose seven men from among you who are known to be full of the Spirit and wisdom. We will turn this responsibility over to them and will give our attention to prayer and the ministry of the word. (6: 1-4)
The church . . . grew in numbers. (9: 31)	The church . . . was strengthened and encouraged by the Holy Spirit . . . living in the fear of the Lord. (9: 31)
The Lord's hand was with them, and a great number of people believed and turned to the Lord. (11: 21)	The disciples, each according to his ability, decided to provide help for the brothers living in Judea. This they did, sending their gift to the elders by Barnabas and Saul. (11: 29, 30)

The Church: God's agent

Luke begins Acts by saying that his former book (the Gospel of Luke) had dealt with "all that Jesus began to do and to teach until the day he was taken up to heaven" (1: 1, 2). He thus implies that the Book of Acts is "The Greatest Story Ever Told—Part II," the story of what Jesus continued to do and teach through his Church. The same Spirit that came upon Jesus when he was baptized, empowering him for his mission (Luke 3: 21, 22), is now upon the Church, empowering believers to continue Jesus' mission (Acts 1: 8).

God's evangelist is the whole Body of Christ, not just the specially gifted communicator!

Why is it important to understand that the total Church is the agent of evangelism?

First, authentic Christian community is in itself a powerful witness. Jesus made clear that "all men will know that you are my disciples if you love one another" (John 13: 35). Love is not the only test of discipleship, but it is the final badge. Love for other believers authenticates our discipleship and makes the message of Jesus credible to the watching world.

Jesus' first little band of disciples was a model of his ability to reconcile people of sharply varying backgrounds. John and Peter were of opposite temperaments, one an idealistic dreamer, the other an impetuous activist. Simon the Zealot was a member of the underground, a revolutionary who wanted to overthrow Roman occupation. Matthew, on the other hand, was a collaborator with the Romans. Before they met Jesus, Simon would have gladly slit Matthew's throat in a back alley! But in Christ they became one.

The church at Antioch, which sent out the first cross-cultural missionary team, was a remarkable microcosm of the ancient world. According to Acts 13: 1, its leadership included Barnabas the Levite, Simeon called Niger (which literally means "black"), Lucius of Cyrene, Manaen (an aristocrat), and Saul the former Pharisee. Two Jews, two Africans, and a royal consort found a new center of gravity in Jesus.

Without deep caring, the words we say about Jesus' peace will ring rather hollow. But with God-given *koinonia,* we can expect people to be drawn to the Body of Christ.

Recently a young man picked me up to go to a meeting in Los Angeles. I discovered that he was Jewish and had moved to California from Canada several years before. He had become very successful in business, yet was conscious of an inner void in his life. A girl invited him to go with her to church. "I don't remember a thing the preacher said the first Sunday," he told me. "In fact, I couldn't tell you anything he said for several weeks. But I kept coming back because I was so impressed with the way these people related to each other, with a warmth and love and quality of caring to which I was a stranger. Finally it hit me that what the man in the pulpit was talking about was the reason for this love. And," he finished, "that's what brought me to Jesus Christ."

The world today is starved for community. We live in a nation of strangers, characterized by empty homes, lonely faces, and alienation. Our greatest social problem may be loneliness. A rediscovery of the fellowship of the Holy Spirit will be a powerful tool for sharing our faith.

Many of our churches have become exclusive clubs for hothouse saints instead of hospitals for sinners. A friend of mine told me of a sad experience when he was chairman of the Billy Graham crusade in Boston. One night a highly paid call girl went forward and accepted Christ. She was employed by a large corporation to "entertain" clients. The pastor in charge of crusade follow-up mentioned later that this girl had started to attend his church.

"Is she going to make it?" asked my friend.

The pastor replied, "Oh, she'll make it, but I'm not sure my church will." He confessed that the people, knowing of her past, mainly left her alone.

We Christians sometimes talk in glowing terms about "winning the world to Christ." Actually, we know the whole world will not be converted. But suppose it were? What would a world "won to Christ" be like? Would its personal relationships be like those in your church and mine? Would its educational system be patterned after our Sunday schools? Would its political and economic systems operate like the governing boards of our churches? These questions are not meant to send us on a guilt trip, for there is no perfect church. (If there were, you and I couldn't join it!) But they should make us ask whether our local fellowship is, in any genuine sense, a prototype of the Kingdom of God.

A true Christian community provides the atmosphere in which disciples are nurtured, strengthened, and have their gifts identified and developed. Each of us has strengths as well as weaknesses. We need each other. That's one reason God has not left us as "lone-ranger" Christians but has placed us in his family.

For a fascinating Bible study, take the phrases *one another* and *each other* to see how often they appear in the New Testament. For example:

"Love each other" (John 15: 17).

"Honor one another" (Rom. 12: 10).

"Accept one another" (Rom. 15: 7).

"Have equal concern for each other" (1 Cor. 12: 25).

"Serve one another" (Gal. 5: 13).

"Be kind and compassionate to one another" (Eph. 4: 32).

"Submit to one another" (Eph. 5: 21).

"Encourage each other" (1 Thess. 4:18).

"Pray for each other" (James 5:16).

This is the "Church of One Another." It's a church where we accept each other as we are, a church marked not by put-downs but by build-ups. In this atmosphere we can find the security to speak the truth to each other, our rough edges can be smoothed, and our latent spiritual gifts can grow.

Putting God's gifts to use

At the 1974 Lausanne conference on evangelism mentioned earlier, theologian Howard Snyder emphasized that the Bible does not see the church primarily as an institution but as a community that works with the sharing of gifts. We receive our Christian life as a gift from God, because we are saved by grace (Greek word: *charis*) through faith. God continues to give spiritual gifts *(charismata)* by which the church is built up. The structures, forms, and institutions of the church change from culture to culture and age to age. The thing that endures is this "body life." We have to constantly reexamine the programs of the church to make sure that they are effective vehicles for expressing the spiritual gifts God gives to believers. "Fellowship and community life are necessary," emphasized Snyder, "in order to prepare Christians for witness and service."[1]

In a witty and provocative address, a Latin American pastor described how his church had fleshed out this theory. He was working hard and church attendance was growing, but he noticed that when he relaxed, the church shrank. He began to pray and fast about the problem. A conviction grew that his church was not growing, just getting fatter! "We used to have two hundred members without love," he said. "Then the number grew to six hundred—still without love." Converts were being added, but disciples were not being multiplied.

He also realized that they didn't really have a church—God's family—but rather an orphanage of which the pastor was the director. The people came to church in a mass, sat down, and he fed them milk. He began to see that in genuine evangelism all God's people and not just the pastors are to be reproducing spiritual life.

The pastor and the spiritual leaders of his church went out to the country for two or three days. When they came back, they told the people they would not use the word *member* anymore because it brought to mind a club membership. They did not find the word *member* in the Book of Acts, but they did find the word *disciple*. So they started using that term. On a one-to-one basis and in small groups they began to disciple and teach through specific, personal direction.

After nearly two years of this, they rediscovered the word *member* in the Epistles. Now it had an entirely different meaning. It meant not members of a club, but members of a body. Just as the wrist joins the arm with the hand, so each member of the Body of Christ passes nourishment and instruction to others.

A primary function of the Christian body is to identify the gifts of the members and to equip them for ministry. In the major passages dealing with spiritual gifts—Romans 12, 1 Corinthians 12, Ephesians 4—the context emphasizes the life of the Christian community. Ephesians 4:11, 12, for example, clearly states that the leaders—apostles, prophets, evangelists, pastors, and teachers—are to prepare all of God's people for service and to bring the whole body to maturity.

This has revolutionary implications. Biblically, every believer is a minister. My friend Lloyd Ogilvie, pastor of First Presbyterian Church of Hollywood, refuses to let the people in the church call him or the pastoral staff *ministers*. When someone designates him that way, Ogilvie gently reminds him that he and the staff are *pastors;* the people are the *ministers*.

Evangelists in the New Testament included what we today would call professionals—apostles and others who were ordained. When Jesus chose his twelve men, one of the primary requirements was that they should be with him and that he would send them forth to preach. These apostles were the wandering evangelists, the advance troops who traveled from city to city to win converts. The pastors and teachers who settled in one area also engaged in evangelism. Paul told the elders in the Ephesian church to follow his own evangelistic example of witnessing from house to house. It is interesting that the theologians and philosophers of the day also regarded themselves as evangelists. Pantaenus, trained as a Stoic philosopher, was converted to Christianity and wandered around gathering crowds of hearers for public debates with pagan thinkers. We could use more Christian intellectuals today who would see themselves as evangelists!

But evangelism was not carried out mainly by the professionals. Historian Adolph Harnack claimed that "the great mission of Christianity was in reality accomplished by informal missionaries."[2] In Acts 8, it was not the apostles but the "amateur" missionaries who were scattered abroad from Jerusalem by the persecution that arose when Stephen was martyred. They spread the gospel as they traveled.

According to Michael Green, "This must often have been not formal preaching but the informal chattering to friends and chance acquaintances, in homes and wine shops, on walks, and around market stalls. They went everywhere gossiping the gospel; they did it naturally, enthusiastically, and with the conviction of those who were not paid to say that sort of thing. Consequently, they were taken seriously, and the movement spread, notably among the lower classes."[3]

Archaeologists digging in the remains of a school for imperial pages in Rome found a picture dating from the third century. It shows a boy standing, his hand raised, worshiping a figure on a cross, a figure that looks like a man with the head of an ass. Scrawled in the writing of a young person are the words, "Alexamenos worships his God." Nearby is a second inscription: "Alexamenos is faithful." Apparently, a young man who was a Christian was being mocked by his schoolmates for his faithful witness. But he was not ashamed; he was faithful.

Women played a major part in the early Christian movement. In fact, on many occasions women were the first to tell about Jesus. The Samaritan woman, whose encounter at the well with Jesus is described in John 4, went back to the town and said, "Come, see a man who told me everything I ever did. Could this be the Christ?" (vs. 29).

It has been pointed out that when Jesus died, women were last at the cross; and when he arose, they were first at the empty tomb. They were the first to tell the apostles that Jesus had risen (Luke 24: 9). The first convert to Christianity in Europe was a woman named Lydia (Acts 16), and the first European church started was a home-church meeting in her residence. Just as there was no distinction between "laymen" and "professionals," there was no distinction between the sexes in evangelism in the early church. Michael Green points out that this continued in the second century, sometimes through public speaking and sometimes through martyrdom. "The preaching of a Maximilla, Thecla, or the four daughters of the Philippian evangelist had a power which was not to be denied."[4]

But across the centuries, the New Testament pattern was obscured. A hierarchy developed in which the ministers were those who were trained and paid to do the work of Christ. Until very recently, the attitude of many laymen has been that they paid the minister to evangelize, or, if they were especially dedicated, they *helped* the ministers spread the faith.

Ironically, a misplaced comma in the book of Ephesians may be blamed for part of the problem. As I wrote in *The Christian Persuader:*

We have been operating on "the fallacy of the misplaced comma" in the fourth chapter of Ephesians! . . . Most of the older versions and some newer ones translate Ephesians 4: 11 and 12 in this sense: "And his gifts were that some should be apostles, some prophets, some evangelists, some pastors and teachers, for the equipment of the saints, for the work of the ministry, for building up the body of Christ." . . . Actually, there should be no comma between these first two phrases. Even a different preposition is used. In "for the equipment of the saints" it is *pros,* while in "for the work of the ministry" it is *eis*—or, as it would be better to say, "unto the work of ministry." A more accurate translation, then, runs: "And these were his gifts: some to be apostles, some prophets, some evangelists, some pastors and teachers, to equip God's people for work in his service. . . . " Or as Phillips correctly paraphrases, "His gifts were made that Christians might be properly equipped for their service."

The error is a small one in grammar, but a great one in practical consequences. For it now appears that the clergy's main task is not to do the work of the Church, but to equip God's people to do this work. The clergyman still has a particular ministry—evangelizing or shepherding or teaching. But this is a means to fulfill his main business: preparing Christians to serve.

In terms of evangelism, the old pattern will not do. It is not enough for the layman to pay the preacher to win souls, or even help him to do so. The pattern is that the minister helps the layman to evangelize!

. . . He conceives his main task as that of training the Christian mechanic how to witness in the garage; as showing the Christian student how to have a relevant testimony in the classroom; as inspiring the Christian housewife to be a godly influence in her neighborhood. As a coach, he learns the talents of each player and fits him in the best spot, so that the whole church becomes an effective witnessing team."[5]

Evangelism and spiritual gifts

Tremendous interest has surfaced today in the whole area of understanding spiritual gifts. This can have a very healthy effect on evangelism if we do not get hung up by the controversy surrounding the more spectacular gifts, such as tongues or healing.

Some Christians have a specific gift, a unique ability from God to present the gospel message and to call people to a decision. I believe this is the gift Paul refers to in Ephesians 4: 11. I like to think of these people as "switch-throwers." God uses them in a unique way to throw the switch and make spiritual light flood into people's minds and souls.

Many more Christians have this gift than we realize. In our Christian groups we need to identify these people and help them to use their gift.

Not all Christians, however, are gifted as switch-throwers. We also need to stress that every spiritual gift is useful in sharing the good news. Read the following list (condensed from Howard Snyder's Lausanne address) and think about your own gift and how it is best used.

1. Some believers can exercise a public ministry of evangelism through proclamation. These include cross-cultural missionaries, evangelists, and many pastors and lay people with the gift of public communication.

2. Large numbers of individual believers can share their faith both by loving deeds and by verbal expression as they are trained and equipped to do so.

3. Some people have gifts useful in building up the inner life of the church. Examples would be teachers, those who give, and those with the gift of administration. They provide the spiritual, organizational, and financial framework for the work of evangelism.

4. These same gifts can be used to welcome, teach, and nurture new Christians.

5. As all the gifts work harmoniously together, the Body gives to the world a living demonstration that the gospel is true.

Can you think of other ways in which spiritual gifts are useful in sharing our faith?

Recently a seminary student met an airline pilot who seemed particularly unhappy. The student asked him if he was a believer. He replied that he was, and that he knew he had eternal life, but that he was miserable because of his failure in sharing his faith. He said, "I've tried to lead the other pilots to Christ. I've tried to lead the mechanics to Christ, the reservation clerks, and management. I haven't succeeded with a single one. As a matter of fact, no one wants to fly with me!"

The student said, "Well, you obviously don't have the gift of being an evangelist."

"What's that?" asked the pilot.

The student repeated himself, and the pilot answered, "No, I sure don't."

"Well, what gift do you have?" asked the student. When the pilot said he didn't understand, the seminarian asked him what he enjoyed doing.

"Well, down at the church," said the pilot, "not many of them are practical. When a door comes off the hinges, I like to hang it back in place. I like to do the repairs around the place, especially since I have a lot of time off."

The student then said, "Let me tell you something—the Lord has given you a valuable gift, the gift of aids. I expect to meet a lot of people in this city while I am in school. Would you like me to call you if I hear about a special need? I don't care what you do about it. Would you just like to know about it?"

The pilot said he would, and for the next year this student referred many special needs to him. The student told me later that to his knowledge, seven out of every ten needs were somehow met, either by the pilot or someone he recruited. Meanwhile, the pilot became one of the happiest Christians he had ever seen.

Unwrapping our gifts

Paul wrote to Timothy to remind him "to fan into flame the gift of God, which is in you through the laying on of my hands" (2 Tim. 1:6).

That admonition tells us three important things about our gifts: they are *initiated* by God, *mediated* through other believers, and *stimulated* by our own faith and obedience. Spiritual gifts are "the gift of God." He takes the initiative in assigning them. In 1 Corinthians 12, Paul teaches that God has given many diverse gifts to the church, and that the Holy Spirit "gives them to each man, just as he determines" (vs. 11). He goes on to say, "God has arranged the parts in the body, every one of them, just as he wanted them to be" (vs. 18). We don't choose our spiritual gift. God decides what gifts the body needs and assigns one or more gifts to each believer to meet that need. In the New Testament these were *speaking* gifts—for example, prophecy, teaching, evangelism; or *service* gifts—for example, liberality and helps; or *sign* gifts—for example, miracles, healing, and tongues. It is stimulating and encouraging to realize that God holds us responsible for the development and use of the gifts he gives us, not for those he doesn't give us.

Spiritual gifts are also *mediated* to us by other believers. Paul told Timothy that his gift was received "through the laying on of my hands." This gesture is usually seen as a formal act in which people are set aside for a specific ministry. However, I would like to suggest that we can also take it in an informal sense, as anything that helps us identify and discover our gifts. Sometimes it helps just to go to another Christian and encourage him to use a gift we have noticed that he may still be unaware of.

Every gift is special. And it's important to honor especially those that seem to be "lesser" gifts or not as spectacular. Paul compares the Body of Christ to the physical body: "those parts of the body that seem to be weaker are indispensable, and the parts that we think are less honorable we treat with special honor" (1 Cor. 12:22, 23).

As an individual, I have the responsibility to *stimulate,* to "fan into flame the gift of God." Just as we use a poker to stir up a fire, so we must probe, study, and observe in order to discover these spiritual gifts. We must study the Scriptures so we will know what the gifts are. We ought also to observe these gifts in the actions of other Christians. In fact, the way we usually discover our gift is to see another Christian exercising a particular gift and then to feel drawn toward the same gift ourselves. As we try to use that gift, we will probably find both fulfillment for ourselves and blessing for others. If so, this is confirmation that we have found a gift God has given us.

As a boy of sixteen, I first met Billy Graham and other gifted evangelists through the Youth for Christ movement. Observing these men and women in action, both personally and publicly, I felt something stirring within me. A longing to express my faith grew. Opportunities came to speak at youth groups and then at small evangelistic occasions. People were moved to accept Christ through what I said. While I believe God has given me certain other spiritual gifts, the gift of evangelism is primary. And I have discovered that it is only as I fan it into flame that I find fulfillment and growth in other areas of my Christian life.

But there is also a particular danger in emphasizing spiritual gifts. People sometimes become so specialized that they say, "Well, I don't share my faith because that is not my gift."

Every Christian has responsibilities that are not always related to gifts. For example, according to Romans 12, some people have particular gifts of "serving," of "encouraging," and of "contributing to the needs of others." Yet each of us is responsible to serve, to encourage, and to contribute liberally, even though these are not our particular spiritual gifts. Or take the gift of "faith" (1 Cor. 12: 9). Those with this gift are people entrusted by God with particular vision to pioneer in certain areas, to see the unseen. Yet it would be ridiculous for me to say, "I don't have the gift of faith, so I won't live by faith." All Christians have the responsibility to walk by faith regardless of whether they have a gift in this area.

So we must not use the teaching of spiritual gifts as a cop-out to avoid our responsibility to share Christ with others. You may not be called as an evangelist, but you and every Christian, by an attitude of love, by compassionate concern, and by well-chosen words, can have the privilege to lead others—perhaps many others—toward Jesus Christ.

My wife has two brothers. One is Billy Graham, world evangelist. The other is Melvin Graham, farmer. Melvin is a committed Christian who seeks to witness for the Lord. Suppose that Billy should preach for another thirty-two years. During each of those years he would hold five major evangelistic crusades, and in each there would be an average of ten thousand conversions. In thirty-two years, more than a million and a half people would come to Christ. What a tremendous advance for the gospel!

But suppose that during the next year Melvin Graham was used by God to lead one person to Jesus Christ. Suppose that the next year he would help this new Christian to grow, and each of them would lead one more to Christ. The next year

those four would win four more. If that group continued dou-
bling every year, in thirty-two years it would number more than
four *billion* people—approximately the population of the world
today!

That's chain-reaction sharing. But, you object, that process of
multiplication will break down some place. Perhaps so. But at
least it helps us catch the vision of what could happen if each of
us said, "Lord, take me, use me, fill me. And let your people
grow!"

1.   J. D. Douglas, ed., *Let the Earth Hear His Voice* (Minneapolis: World Wide,
1975), p. 333.
2.   Adolph Harnack, *The Mission and Expansion of Christianity in the First Three
Centuries* (Gloucester, Mass.: Peter Smith), p. 368.
3.   Green, *Evangelism in the Early Church,* p. 173.
4.   Green, *Evangelism in the Early Church,* p. 176.
5.   Ford, *The Christian Persuader,* pp. 48-49.

7

How the Good News Travels

Each person's spiritual journey is a lifelong decision process. It may begin many years prior to the point when a decision is made and one becomes born again, or regenerated, in the Biblical sense.

The responsibility of the Christian communicator is to approach people where they are in terms of their spiritual position and, through an appropriate combination of message and media, to cause them to progress in their decision process toward initial commitment and subsequent growth.[1]
— James F. Engel and H. Wilbert Norton

WHAT ACTUALLY GOES ON inside a person who accepts the good news? Is it a mysterious alchemy that defies analysis? Or can we spell out the specifics of what happens first, second, third?

Dr. James Engel, formerly a marketing professor at Ohio State University, spent years figuring out what seems to motivate people to buy products. More recently, he and his colleagues at the Wheaton College Graduate School in Illinois have taken a similar long look at the process of evangelism. Dr. Engel and H. Wilbert Norton, dean of the school, have written a book entitled *What's Gone Wrong with the Harvest?*, to which I am indebted for many of the ideas in this chapter.

They suggest that the Great Commission's command to

THE SPIRITUAL-DECISION PROCESS

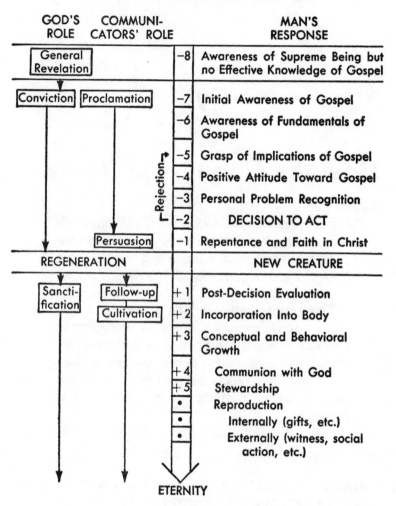

GOD'S ROLE	COMMUNI-CATORS' ROLE		MAN'S RESPONSE
General Revelation		−8	Awareness of Supreme Being but no Effective Knowledge of Gospel
Conviction	Proclamation	−7	Initial Awareness of Gospel
		−6	Awareness of Fundamentals of Gospel
		−5	Grasp of Implications of Gospel
		−4	Positive Attitude Toward Gospel
		−3	Personal Problem Recognition
		−2	DECISION TO ACT
	Persuasion	−1	Repentance and Faith in Christ
REGENERATION			NEW CREATURE
Sancti-fication	Follow-up	+1	Post-Decision Evaluation
	Cultivation	+2	Incorporation Into Body
		+3	Conceptual and Behavioral Growth
		+4	Communion with God
		+5	Stewardship
		•	Reproduction
		•	Internally (gifts, etc.)
		•	Externally (witness, social action, etc.)

Rejection

ETERNITY

make disciples contains three mandates that are related but distinct:

1. to proclaim the message
2. to persuade the unbeliever
3. to cultivate the believer.

They have attempted to diagram the process by which the gospel is communicated and a person becomes a disciple (see page 86). The authors make no claim that this is a final and definitive statement. The Holy Spirit works as he will (John 3: 8). But this is a helpful tool in describing how the good news travels from A to B.

If your own coming to Christ is recent enough that you can remember the stages clearly, compare it to this diagram. If you are presently trying to share Christ with certain people, try to think through where they are on the scale.*

Jesus: the model communicator

Learning to be good communicators throughout this process does *not* mean we have to steep ourselves in Madison Avenue techniques. Actually, the more we learn of what works in communication, the more we realize that Jesus was the best.

Matthew's Gospel tells us at the very beginning that Jesus' name was to be "Immanuel," which means "God with us" (1: 23). Jesus was the presence of God among men, God's full and bodily identification with our human condition. Jesus wasn't playing pretend, wearing a kind of human disguise. He was baptized by John in the Jordan River (3: 13), thus identifying with our sin and need of cleansing even though he himself had no sin. He was tempted by the devil (4: 1), thus identifying with trials we all face. He was hungry (4: 2); he knew what it was to feel the pangs of physical weakness and suffering. Jesus Christ earned the right to communicate by becoming a man, a servant man, even a suffering man.

We need to take all this seriously. Jesus himself said, "As the Father has sent me, I am sending you" (John 20: 21). When God the Father wanted to save the world, how did he do it? He

---

*In the light of Scripture and personal experience you may want to try drawing your own model. I would personally prefer, for example, to have Regeneration begin at least at -2 (Decision to Act) and perhaps even at -3 or -4. This is because I believe that man cannot make that decision to act, repent, and believe without God's enabling power.

didn't shout from heaven. He didn't even send a tape recording. He sent his Son into the world.

Some wall graffiti at the University of Wisconsin read, "God isn't dead; he just doesn't want to get involved." But God did get involved. The Word did not become words; he "became flesh and lived for a while among us" (John 1: 14). He even died for the world. No miraculous escape turned up at the last moment. Indeed, "God made him . . . to be sin for us" (2 Cor. 5: 21). His was a complete identification—in birth, in life, and in death.

Our disciple-making must fit this incarnational pattern. No matter how much information we have and how many techniques we learn, there is no way we can really be effective in communication and remain uninvolved with people.

From presence to proclamation

Our Christian presence in the world, of course, is not enough. Some people say, "You can talk about Jesus if you want. I don't talk about my faith; I just live it." That sounds good, but it misses two very important points. The first is that none of us is good enough to let just our lives speak for Christ. We have to use words to point beyond ourselves. The second is that even Jesus Christ, though he was the perfect and sinless Son of God, didn't stop at presence. "From that time on Jesus began to preach, 'Repent, for the kingdom of heaven is near' " (Matt. 4: 17). It is worth remembering that it wasn't until he left his carpenter shop and went out to teach and preach that people heard the good news. A familiar Chinese proverb says, "One picture is worth a thousand words"—and yet it takes words to say that! Sharing our faith always involves speaking in some way, just as it also always means a total relationship involving more than just saying words.

I don't think Jesus' example necessarily means that we walk up to people and say to them out of the blue, "The kingdom of heaven is at hand." The very idea of a king doesn't mean much to the average person. So we have to understand where people are and, if necessary, interpret and translate our message in terms and ideas they can grasp.

But it remains important for us to understand that we really are talking about people getting to know God. The well-known

Christian philosopher Francis Schaeffer says that the first part of the gospel message today is not "Jesus died for your sins" but "God is really there." He doesn't mean that the message of the cross is unimportant. He means that people won't understand the cross or Jesus or salvation until they realize they are made for God and their basic need is reconciliation to him.

Sometimes our evangelism has been cheap. We have stressed Jesus as a personal Savior who meets people's needs without presenting him as the Lord of the universe who demands their surrender.

"God is like Coke—he's the real thing."

"God is like Pan Am—he makes the going great."

"God is like Pepsi—he's got a lot to give."

"God is like Alka-Seltzer—try him, you'll like him."

"God is like aspirin—he takes the pain away."

"God is like Tide—he gets the stain the others leave behind."

"God is like Frosted Flakes—he's gr-r-r-eat."

No doubt the Christians who use such slogans mean well. But to present Jesus Christ in that way is very dangerous. If we leave the holy Creator-God out of the picture, we shouldn't be surprised to end up with shallow converts who have "accepted Jesus" but whose lives have never changed.

The first gospel presentation I learned as a boy started with man's sin; "All have sinned and come short of the glory of God" (Rom. 3:23, KJV). In contrast, the first of Campus Crusade's Four Spiritual Laws is "God loves you and has a wonderful plan for your life." The first of the Billy Graham Association's Steps to Peace with God is "God loves you and wants you to experience peace and the abundant life." These are great improvements; they start with God, and they start positively.

But maybe the very first step ought rather to be "God is really there. He is in charge. He has a sovereign purpose for all things." At least that's where Jesus started.

From proclamation to communication

Study Jesus, and you will find that he chose his language carefully. *Kingdom* would not be an in word today, but for the people Jesus was talking to it was very meaningful political language. When he chose some fishermen to follow him, he said, "I will make you fishers of men."

Jesus was using what modern communications experts call an "adaptive orientation." This simply means that he communicated with people at the point of their felt needs in terms they could understand. To Nicodemus the ruler, he said, "You must be born again"—he never used "born again," a highly conceptual metaphor, in any other recorded instance in the New Testament. He talked to the woman by the well about "living water." But when the rich young man came up and asked what he had to do to have eternal life, Jesus did not talk to him about living water. Knowing that money was this man's god, he said, "Sell your possessions and give to the poor, and you will have treasure in heaven. Then come, follow me." He was basically calling him to a total switch of gods. On the other hand, he didn't tell Zacchaeus, the tax collector who went up in a tree, to give away everything he had. He simply said, "Zacchaeus . . . I must stay at your house today." By the end of the day, Zacchaeus had decided on his own to give half his possessions to the poor.

The reason we need this adaptive orientation is that people have filters—emotional and intellectual screens through which all incoming messages are fed. Each human being's background, culture, and experience affects his attitudes, personality, and responses. In addition to these natural filters, there are also spiritual filters. We block out messages from God that might interfere with the way we are running our lives. Paul speaks in Romans 1:18 of people "who suppress the truth by their wickedness." The New Testament refers to this often as a kind of spiritual blindness.

Communication research shows that we listen to what we want to hear. This is called selective attention. Furthermore, we get what we want out of what we hear. This is called selective perception. And finally, we remember what we want; this is selective retention.

All of us know people who show no interest or responsiveness to the message of Jesus Christ. Their filters are closed; they feel no need. They are like the rocky, hard ground in Jesus' parable of the soils. On the other hand, people whose filters are open show that they do have a felt need. They are like the open, good ground, receptive to the seed.

If we are really serious about sharing our faith, then we must take time to know people. Jesus did. "He knew what was in a man" (John 2:25). Part of Jesus' knowledge certainly came because he was the unique Son of God. But never forget that he also lived as a man among men. He lived with people. He talked with them. He went to parties and weddings and funerals. He found out where they lived and he met them where they were. And he took them from the known to the unknown.

A crucial need in sharing our faith is being relevant to people. I don't mean that we make the gospel relevant. The gospel *is* relevant. But sometimes we aren't. Just as Jesus did, we have to start where people are and lead them to where God wants them to go. We need to start with what is contemporary and move to biblical truth. Study, experience, intuition, and the leading of the Holy Spirit through prayer will help us put up our spiritual radar until we can locate the people we are trying to reach.

From communication to persuasion

Dr. Ted Ward, Christian scholar and professor at Michigan State University, has said, "Communication is more than telling . . . purposeful communication is the presentation of information in carefully designed form to an appropriate audience through a useful medium in order to produce a change. *Until change results, we haven't gotten through.*"

As we have noted, Jesus' first message was "Repent, for the kingdom of heaven is near."

The word *repent* here is the Greek word *metanoeo* and literally means "to think after" or "to change one's mind." Repentance is a change of attitude, perspective, value, and direction.

The invitations of Jesus always coupled the gracious offer with a costly demand. He offered the kingdom, and demanded a change of mind. He offered a treasure, and demanded that we sell everything to possess it. He offered eternal life, and demanded that we go through a narrow gate. He offered freedom, but demanded submission to his authority. He offered happiness, but demanded a poverty in spirit.

Jesus spelled out in his Beatitudes that if you are unhappy, then you have to start looking at life in a new way, with the mind of Christ, where the main thing is not happiness but righteousness, being right with God, yourself, and others.

There has been a marked tendency in our time to push the positive and soft-pedal the negative when presenting Christ to people. But this overlooks the fact that people don't change unless they recognize the problem in their lives.

Some years ago I was very close to a group of high-school students who were part of a Christian movement in the city where we live. Through the influence of a teacher, several Christian workers, and their peers, scores of young people professed to become Christians. Fifteen years have now passed. Some of these students have grown into real maturity and discipleship. Others very disappointingly have become indifferent and fallen by the wayside or in some cases have even turned hostile to their previous commitment. What happened? One girl told me she had gone forward in an evangelistic meeting because her boyfriend went, and it was not until some years later that she found the reality of Christ for herself. When peer influence changed as they left their high-school group and went to college, it was evident in some cases that they had no real, personal, internal response.

We need to be aware that genuine persuasion has not taken place simply when there is *compliance* with what society or family or church asks, nor when there is merely *identification* with the communicator. Genuine persuasion and changes happen only when the message is *internalized*. Isn't this what Jesus was saying in the parable of the soils? Only in the good ground was the seed, so to speak, "internalized"; it got its roots down into the ground and brought forth fruit.

The message we try to share with others must be applied prayerfully until it touches the sore place in the life of the hearer and brings him to the place of recognizing his problem and need before God.

We also need to recognize that there is a difference between mental assent to the general sinfulness of mankind and a heartfelt desire to change. As my friend Kenneth Chafin, a Houston pastor, points out, if I am in a meeting where the speaker asks all imperfect husbands to stand up, I will stand up along with every other husband, with a bit of a self-conscious twitter. But if on the way home my wife turns to me and says, "Honey, you didn't pay any attention to me tonight. I really felt left out and unwanted," I will feel guilty, ashamed, and hopefully I will do something to change. Why? Because someone I love has touched a sore point, an area of need in my life.

Communication that persuades people to come to Jesus Christ is not the work of human agency alone. Witnessing is not brainwashing. Sharing our faith is not sales technique. Genuine Christian communication is not a matter of cleverness or manipulation. It is a matter of authentically presenting and embodying the message, and prayerfully trusting the Holy Spirit to apply it.

It is helpful to make a distinction in our thinking here between regeneration and conversion. Regeneration, the new birth, is the work of God the Holy Spirit in applying the gospel to people's lives. We cannot observe when or how this takes place; it is the "underside" of the spiritual decision. Conversion, however, is a process we can observe. It is a turning from sin and self-centeredness to God. Paul mentioned that the Thessalonians had "turned to God from idols to serve the living and true God" (1 Thess. 1:9). The conversion experience is not the same with every person. Some people have a very sudden conversion, like a couple who fall in love at first sight. Other people turn to Christ more gradually, like a couple who have grown up next to each other. When they are little kids, he pulls her hair and she scratches his face. Suddenly when they are seventeen he looks at this girl next door and says, "Wow! Where did she come from?" The important thing isn't how quickly these people fall in love but that they do love each other and want to commit their lives to each other.

What is crucial is not whether a conversion experience is dramatic or quiet, gradual or sudden, but that it is a genuine encounter with Jesus Christ that touches the person at every level of his being.

God uses us as human communicators, but he is the one who really does the work. We can talk to people about their need and tell them that "all have sinned," but it is the Holy Spirit who convicts them of sin (John 16:8). We can explain the gospel and try to answer people's questions honestly (for God does not bypass our minds in conversion but rather illuminates them), but it still is the Holy Spirit who convinces people of the truth. "No one can say, 'Jesus is Lord,' except by the Holy Spirit" (1 Cor. 12:3).

Perhaps we can compare this to how rivets are put into the hull of a ship to hold metal plates together. It is impossible for a worker to push the rivet through with his hand. He needs a pneumatic gun. But without the rivets, the gun would just make a hole in the ship. The rivet is like our communication of Jesus Christ to people. The pneumatic gun is like the power of the Holy Spirit. You and I *can* save no one. God *will* save no one unless we are faithful to communicate the gospel, except perhaps in some extraordinary cases in which he may directly communicate without human means.

From persuasion to cultivation

If we are true to Jesus' pattern, evangelism will not end with the decision for Christ. The end product of evangelism is not just a decision but a mature, growing disciple who is able to reproduce and share Christ with others.

According to Matthew 4, Jesus ministered to large crowds of people. He preached. He healed. He taught in the synagogues. But Jesus moved from the crowds to a core group. He called some fishermen to come and follow him. Jesus took them into his fellowship, his work, his community, and his teaching. He was cultivating these men, informing their minds, transforming their life-styles into his own image. He was willing not just to give them a message but to invest his own life, to pour himself into them. For Jesus, discipleship was not a certain point of the process. A disciple was someone moving with Jesus, going for Jesus, following him, fishing for him, learning from him, being his person.

Jesus linked decision and discipleship inseparably in the Great Commission. He said those who became disciples were to be baptized and taught to obey everything he had commanded. As Michael Green comments, there was a "universal and quite unselfconscious link between the invisible encounter of man's faith with God's grace, and its outward expression in baptism."[2] As soon as someone confessed faith in Christ and repented, baptism was administered. The Philippian jailer, for example, was baptized without delay, according to Acts 16. Either before or immediately after baptism, the new converts were also carefully instructed to obey the teachings of Jesus. Green indicates that this instruction was in four categories: (1)

the putting off of the old evil nature, (2) proper Christian submission in the various areas of political and social life, (3) the charge to watch and pray, (4) the need for standing firm in the faith and resisting the assaults of the devil.[3]

Disciple making is a process that does not end until new minds become reshaped in the consciousness of Jesus Christ so that they may be salt and light in the world. We are to commit ourselves to people not only that they might be "born again" but "until Christ is formed in [them]" (Gal. 4:19).

Disciple making calls us to be like Jesus in our presence, our proclamation, our communication, our persuasion, and our cultivation.

Our prayer should be that we imitate John the Baptist; people "heard him speak, and they followed Jesus" (John 1:37, KJV).

1. James F. Engel and H. Wilbert Norton, *What's Gone Wrong with the Harvest?* (Grand Rapids, Mich.: Zondervan, 1975), pp. 46-47.
2. Green, *Evangelism in the Early Church,* p. 152.
3. Green, *Evangelism in the Early Church,* p. 154.

8

The Bible
and the Bullhorn

We express penitence . . . for having sometimes regarded evangelism and social concern as mutually exclusive. Although reconciliation with man is not reconciliation with God, nor is social action evangelism, nor is political liberation salvation, nevertheless we affirm that evangelism and socio-political involvement are both part of our Christian duty. For both are necessary expressions of our doctrines of God and man, our love for our neighbour and our obedience to Jesus Christ. . . . The salvation we claim should be transforming us in the totality of our personal and social responsibilities. Faith without works is dead.
—The Lausanne Covenant, Clause 5

CROSSING HARVARD YARD one day in the early 1970s, a professor met a coed carrying a large Bible. She earnestly recounted how she had come to believe in Jesus Christ as her Savior.

The professor was startled. The last time he had seen her, she was a hard-core militant revolutionary. As she talked, Bible in hand, his mind flashed back to her leading a protest rally with a bullhorn in her hand.

"A Bible for a bullhorn," he mused. Then he wondered to himself if he might someday see that same girl with both a Bible and a bullhorn, one in each hand, calling out again for justice but this time on the basis of her newfound faith.

How does evangelism relate to social justice? Is there any tie between evangelism and apartheid in South Africa, starvation in Bangladesh, or abortion in Boston?

The Christian church has often divided into pietists and activists. The pietists are often caricatured as "soul savers" interested only in getting people into heaven. The activists are the "social reformers," much more concerned to change the structures of society. This polarization has frequently absorbed much of the church's energy. An old New England statute declared that "when two vehicles shall approach the same intersection at the same time, both shall stop and neither shall move until the other has passed." A similar paralysis has often afflicted the church.

But this has begun to change in the last decade. Many deeply concerned with personal evangelism are also committed to seeing the new birth worked out in the total fabric of life. And many who are deeply concerned with social justice are realizing more and more that the prospects are bleak unless people are changed by the power of the gospel of Christ.

The biblical idea of salvation is one of wholeness. Salvation is personal. God calls each of us by name and asks that we put our personal faith in Christ. Salvation is also cosmic. This doesn't mean that everybody is going to be saved; the Bible doesn't teach that. The cosmic dimension means that salvation relates us to a God who has a purpose for the whole wide world. Salvation is for eternity, and it's for now. The eternal life God gives us is a life that begins now with a new relationship to God and goes on forever. The Jesus Christ who died for our sins and to whom we come as Savior is the Lord of the whole universe.

The Great Commission and the Great Commandments
What all of this means is that our Christian mission includes obedience both to the Great Commission ("Go and make disciples") and the Great Commandments ("Love the Lord your God" and "Love your neighbor as yourself"). The commission didn't replace the commandments. It added a new dimension. If I really love my neighbor, then I'm not going to withhold from him the good news of salvation in Jesus Christ.

Equally, if I really love him, I won't stop with giving him just the gospel. I will be concerned for his total well-being.

Evangelism and social concern are both important parts of our Christian responsibility. A crucial Bible passage that shows this is Luke 4: 18, 19. Here, at the very beginning of his ministry, Jesus said that he had been sent to proclaim release to the captives, sight to the blind, and freedom to the oppressed. He also said he had been sent to preach the gospel to the poor. Notice that he didn't say these were all the same. Preaching the gospel to the poor is different from healing the blind, but all were important parts of his mission.

Jesus is the model for our life and witness. "As the Father has sent me, I am sending you," he said (John 20: 21). We should be as concerned as he was both to preach the gospel that brings forgiveness and eternal salvation and to heal and release people from all that binds and oppresses them.

The question often arises: if evangelism and social action are both important, which has priority?

This is not an easy question. If we have to choose, eternal salvation is more important. An example of this is the story in John, chapter 6, of Jesus feeding the crowd with five loaves and two fish. The people were so impressed they said, "What a great king this man would make." Jesus knew they were intending to make him king by force, so he withdrew to the hills. When the people found him, Jesus said, "You are looking for me, not because you saw miraculous signs but because you ate the loaves and had your fill. Do not work for food that spoils, but for food that endures for eternal life, which the Son of Man will give you" (John 6: 26, 27). Jesus refused to go into the bakery business! He refused to take political power to himself. Clearly he gave priority to eternal life over bread for the body.

Yet Jesus did not drive a wedge between the two. He preached the gospel to the poor and he fed the hungry. Some people will say, "Well, if people who don't hear the gospel are going to be damned and go to hell forever, then our clearest priority must be evangelism." That's a powerful argument. Jesus taught more about hell than anyone. But that did not stop him from opening blind eyes, making paralyzed limbs whole, and feeding empty stomachs that would die and decay in a few short years. Preaching the gospel and healing the sick were both parts of what his Father sent him to do, and he had time for both.

The argument about whether evangelism or social action should have priority often overlooks a crucial point. There is really only one priority in our Christian lives: to do all to the glory of God. Which of these is more important: worshiping God in fellowship on Sunday? Doing my work well on Monday? Sharing the gospel with a friend? Or visiting a prisoner and helping him get a job? *All* of these are important parts of being a Christian—fellowship, service, worship, ministry, and evangelism. But the one priority is to love God with all my heart, to glorify him, and at any given moment do the specific thing that will express his love to my neighbor.

Some practical implications

What does all this mean in the way we share the good news? First, it means we must seriously present the call to repentance and discipleship. Before people accept Jesus, we must emphasize what this repentance and Lordship entails. We have no right to offer cheap grace, putting the offer of eternal life in bold print and the demands of discipleship in small print. The one who saves also asks that we forsake all other lords and follow him. We are asking people to believe on the *Lord* Jesus Christ, to be a part of the community of believers, and to follow his teachings in family life, racial attitudes, sexual life, business ethics, and responsibilities as citizens.

This doesn't mean I have to know every detail about following Jesus or maturing as a Christian before I become one. After I come to Christ, I have to be taught to obey all things he has commanded (Matt. 28: 20). And it doesn't mean that I am going to live a perfect, sinless life after I am born again. What it does mean is that I cannot consciously and persistently reject Jesus' Lordship in some area. When I accept Jesus, I know it costs nothing because of what he did *for* me. But I know it will cost everything because of what he is going to do *in* me. It involves an unconditional commitment to follow Jesus as the implications of his Lordship become clear to me day by day and year after year. Forgiveness without repentance and discipleship is not the gospel.

"But," someone asks, "what does this do to the idea of

grace? If we tell people they have to stop being racists to become Christians, isn't this being saved by works?" Not at all. First, Jesus clearly put repentance and faith together (Mark 1:15). Repentance and faith are like the negative and positive poles of a battery, or two sides of the same coin. Repentance is turning from sin, and faith is turning toward God; one is impossible without the other.

Christians have always said that when people come to Jesus, they have to stop lying and committing adultery. If that is not inconsistent with the doctrine of salvation by grace through faith, then neither is turning from racism and social sins. As Ron Sider says, "Evangelists regularly preach that coming to Jesus means forsaking pot, pubs, and pornography. Too often in this century, however, they have failed to add that coming to Jesus ought to involve repentance of and conversion from the sin of involvement in social evils such as economic injustice and institutionalized racism."

Secondly, our sharing of the faith ought to involve genuine service. We don't serve people just to get them to believe in Jesus, to bribe them into becoming what missionaries in China called "rice Christians." We serve them because they are made in the image of God and we have compassion for them. Our love and service are unconditional, not based on whether they respond to the gospel. But genuine service, offered freely in the name of Christ, will often attract people who otherwise might not be interested. It is estimated that some 25 percent of the Christians in India received their first exposure to Christianity through medical missions.

In Sioux Falls, South Dakota, the First Baptist Church began a halfway house where men released from the prison could live for a nominal rent until they could get jobs. One parolee in his thirties had been in reform school or prison every year since his mid-teens. One day as he sat in the living room, the three-year-old daughter of the couple in charge crawled up in his lap, put her arms around his neck, and gave him a hug. With tears rolling down his cheeks, he said, "You know, this is the first time I can remember anybody touching me in love." A few weeks later that man publicly expressed his commitment to Jesus Christ as Lord and Savior. God used that touch of love to break the scars of all those years.

Third, the vital link between our Christian evangelism and social responsibility is the church itself. Jesus didn't begin a new political party in order to destroy the kingdom of Satan. Instead, he called together a little band of disciples who were committed to him, to each other, and to the Kingdom of God.

Theologian John Yoder believes that "the primary social structure through which the gospel works to change other structures is the Christian community."[1] The community of God's people, living under the cross, is a model of the Kingdom of God on earth. The church can give society no greater gift than to function as the church where the gospel is preached, where people are born again and renewed in the mind of Christ, where they support each other in living for Christ, and from which they move out to act as salt and light in a decaying secular society.

This kind of Christian action is taking shape in many forms throughout the world. One of the most exciting is the Voice of Calvary ministry in rural Mississippi. This unique Christian community has been led by John Perkins, a black man, who left Mississippi after his brother was shot by a policeman. John moved to California, where he prospered in business. He and his wife had little interest in Christ and his church until their little boy began attending a mission Sunday school. The child's songs and stories about Jesus led them to commit their lives to Christ. Then they felt God calling them back to Mississippi for a special ministry, a dangerous move during the civil rights struggle of the 1950s. As Child Evangelism workers, they went into a rural area about thirty miles east of Jackson and taught thousands of students about Jesus each month. Perkins attended various civil rights meetings but was disturbed because the movement had no real base. He was especially concerned that the welfare system was exploiting poor people, turning them into exploiters without raising creative leadership. So he called the leaders of the black community together. Sitting on his porch one evening, they laid plans for a creative new ministry that became the Voice of Calvary.

Central to this community is the evangelistic work of winning young people to Christ—training them as disciples, sending them to school, and calling them back to their own community for service. Part of the Voice of Calvary is a church based on a disciple-making ministry that is pastored by a young man Perkins led to Christ. It also has high-school students tutoring younger children. Co-ops provide an economic base for people to sell and share the crops they produce. Their excellent medical facility has an outstanding program of preventive medicine under which doctors worship in rural churches, gain the confidence of leaders, bring important information about nutrition and child care to expectant mothers, and help to establish Bible studies.

There have been financial struggles, misunderstandings, and hostility even from fellow Christians in building this community. But more and more, the Voice of Calvary has become a model—a city set on a hill that shows the healing gospel of Christ.

The real issue

A few years ago I would have said the question was whether we can get the proper balance between personal evangelism and social action. I now think that is only part of a bigger issue: does our evangelism have the power to make disciples? Is the born-again experience we hear so much about really producing Kingdom men and women? Or does it simply help us pursue "success" in the world system? Does the gospel we proclaim focus so much on the offer of peace of mind that it minimizes gospel demands? Or does it stress changing the central motivation of our lives from getting to giving? In short, does the encounter with Jesus Christ imprint Christ the servant on our minds and values?

Jesus demonstrated that the power and relevance of the gospel depends on faith and obedience, not on our strategy, efficiency, or success. God asks us to follow the Lamb, who was slain and is now changing the world. We are to be faithful to him.

A Young Life staff member working in the Boston inner city was asked, "What do you expect to change?"

His answer was "Anyone who comes to work in the inner city expecting to change it is a fool. I am here because Jesus Christ put me here."

The Christian impact depends on our being a "third race." In the early days of the church, Christians were called just that. People said they were neither Jews nor Gentiles but a third race.

They were marked by a style of life, mind-set, and values so different they were unique.

This doesn't mean we have an identifiable evangelical position on all issues. It does mean that our actions and attitudes will ultimately be judged in the light of the cross.

Jesus began his ministry by proclaiming good news to the poor, healing to the brokenhearted, liberty to the captives, and freedom to the oppressed. He ended it three years later, poor, brokenhearted, captive, and oppressed. If that was defeat, we should turn from him. But if victory, we should drink from that same cup so we might share in his joy.

1.   John Yoder, *The Politics of Jesus* (Grand Rapids, Mich.: Eerdmans, 1972), p. 157.

9

Building Bridges

"I stand by the door," he wrote.
"I neither go too far in, nor stay too far out.
The door is the most important door in the world—
It is the door through which men walk when they find God . . .
Men die outside that door, as starving beggars die
On cold nights, in cruel cities, in the dead of winter—
Nothing else matters compared to helping them find it,
And open it, and walk in, and find Him . . .
So I stand by the door . . .

You can go in too deeply and stay in too long,
And forget the people outside the door,
As for me, I shall take my old accustomed place,
Near enough to God to hear Him, and know He is there,
But not so far from men as not to hear them,
And remember they are there, too.
Where? Outside the door—
Thousands of them, millions of them.
But—more important for me—
One of them, two of them, ten of them,
Whose hands I am intended to put on the latch.
So I shall stand by the door and wait
For those who seek it.
'I had rather be a door-keeper . . .'
So I stand by the door."[1]
                    —Sam Shoemaker, Episcopal rector and evangelist

HOW WOULD YOU DESCRIBE a tree to someone who had never seen one? If you were a philosopher, you might write an 800-page book on "treeness." But if you were an artist, you would likely solve this communication problem by drawing a single tree.

God may be more like an artist than a philosopher. When he wanted to make his ultimate communication of love, truth, and grace, he chose to do it through one solitary life. At a specific point in space and time, Jesus of Nazareth was born, laughed, ate, wept, ran splinters into his finger, and was "the radiance of God's glory and the exact representation of his being" (Heb. 1: 3).

This person-to-person element in Christian sharing is crucial. Amazing as it may seem, God has chosen my life to be a "letter from Christ" that other people can read and know (2 Cor. 3: 2, 3). Christian psychiatrist John White has said, "Witnessing is not putting on a Christian front so as to convince prospective customers. Witnessing is being honest, that is, being true to a God who has made you in your speech and in your day-by-day behavior."[2]

Jesus told his disciples, "You will receive power when the Holy Spirit comes on you; and you will *be* my witnesses . . ." (Acts 1: 8, italics added). Witnessing is not merely an activity that we do at a special time; witnessing is the sum total of all we are, say, and do—a life-style. When Jesus said we were to be the "light of the world," he didn't imply that evangelism was to be a light bulb that is switched on and off, but a constantly burning flame.

"Go into all the world," said Jesus. That's hard for me to grasp. I can understand it better if I think of going into all *my worlds* and if I realize that as I go through the normal traffic patterns of daily life, I am Christ's witness. As I walk with God among people, my desire to invite others to come along should be so natural and transparent that often I am not even aware that I am "witnessing." My prayer should be that God will bring across my path those who will sense the gospel in my life and become hungry for Christ.

Sometimes his reality comes across in the most unconscious ways. A non-Christian girl began going to a church for counseling. She was impressed most, she said later, by the way two of the associate pastors talked to their wives on the telephone, not by the direct help she received. The genuine caring and affection she heard convinced her of the gospel's truth.

I can be certain of two things about every person I meet: God loves him, and he has a need. Personal communication means helping each person take the next step toward Christ or in Christ.

To be God's communicator

Before I can be a communicator for God, I must first be *his person*. Healthy sharing grows out of a healthy relationship with God. In that kind of relationship, we are called, as the old song goes, to accentuate the positive and eliminate the negative. On the negative side, I need to ask God to remove anything that would be misleading or harmful and turn others away from him. This doesn't mean that I cannot witness until I am so perfect that I might be mistaken for Gabriel's twin. But it does mean that I must constantly examine my life in the light of God's Word. If my life doesn't speak humbly and honestly of Christ, I'd better take the Jesus bumper sticker off my car.

The positive side is equally important. Some Christians are like mannequins; they don't dance, drink, or smoke. But neither does the dummy; it doesn't do anything! The witnessing life is not merely emptied of questionable or sinful things; it is filled with the love, joy, peace, and longsuffering characteristic of God.

The important thing is not how far we have come but the direction we are growing. A rough and tough contractor in Canada who became a Christian in one of our crusades said in a subsequent testimony, "I'm not what I should be, I'm not what I'm going to be, but I thank God I'm not what I used to be!" Time alone with God in his Word and prayer as well as time with his people in worship and fellowship are essential as we grow to be God's persons.

Nor does the sense of God's presence require a glamorous and glowing testimony. Sometimes his presence is more evident in the low moments of our lives. Susan, a first-semester student at a midwestern university, was homesick, falling behind in her studies, and ready to withdraw. But she was a Christian and wanted to honor the Lord in her life. After Christmas vacation, her roommate announced she had committed her life to Jesus Christ—and that Susan's life had been a major factor. "My life!" Susan responded. "What has there been in my life to make you want to be a Christian? I've been thoroughly depressed and discouraged."

The answer came, "I observed the way you suffered." God's strength showed through her weakness.

God not only wants me to be his person, he *wants me to be me.* This takes us back to an earlier chapter on self-acceptance and learning to realize God has made each of us unique and wants to use us just as we are.

When I went to college, I was a shy, reserved, conservative Canadian. If you don't believe it, just ask my wife! Personal conversation, repartee, and small talk has never come easy to me. But one of the most important lessons I have learned and am still learning is that God doesn't want me to be someone else. If I try, then I am missing the unique thing he wants to do with me. In the Old Testament story, David tried to use Saul's armor but couldn't because it didn't fit him. Each of us has to find the style that is natural and right for our personality. If I am basically shy, I must not use this as an excuse to cut myself off from other people. Instead, I need to realize that God wants me to love people, but in a different way from the extrovert.

God is a God of infinite variety. He doesn't have one way to reach others; he has a million and one ways. There is no one sales technique, no one series of steps to reach everybody. Technique can even become dehumanizing if it becomes an idol rather than a tool. Observe Jesus as he walked among people in the New Testament. Do you find a set form? A technique? An inflexible pattern? Not at all. True, he repeated many of his sayings and parables on different occasions. But in approaching individuals his evangelism was truly personal. He was free to be himself in each situation and to treat each person uniquely.

Leaving the castle

Personal communication means I must also *be a bridge builder.* Too often we have seen the church of Jesus Christ as a kind of castle where we can hide behind walls for security. Occasionally we make an evangelistic foray. We open the castle door, drop it over the moat, send out a raiding party, and get a few more people to bring inside the castle. What a travesty!

Certainly God has called us to be separate from the sins of the world. But separation was never meant to imply isolation. Paul's position on this is often distorted. It is true that Paul asked, "What does a believer have in common with an unbeliever?" and demanded, "Come out from them and be separate" (2 Cor. 6: 15, 17). But that same Paul also wrote, "I have written you in my letter not to associate with sexually immoral people—not at all meaning the people of this world who are immoral. . . . In that case, you would have to leave this world. But now I am writing you that you must not associate with anyone who calls himself a brother but is sexually immoral" (1 Cor. 5: 9-11). Paul tells believers not to associate with professing Christians who are living in blatant sin, but he does not call us to withdraw from our associations with non-Christians. Jesus prayed not that his Father would take Christians out of the world, but that God would protect them from the evil one. "As you sent me into the world, I have sent them into the world" (John 17: 18). The Christian is first called *out* of the world for Christ's salvation and for building up his faith, and then is sent back *into* the world for service and witness.

Jesus is often described as the great High Priest who opened the way to God. The Latin word for *priest* is *pontifex*, which means "bridgemaker." By dying, Jesus, the bridge builder, opened the way for us to come into God's presence (1 Pet. 3: 18). Now Jesus has sent us to be bridge builders as he was.

Bridge builders have a genuine concern for people. Sometimes my biggest problem in witnessing is being so involved in my own affairs that I don't have time to think of others. Jesus was "other-person centered," the man for others, and we are called to be so. If we see witnessing as going around looking for someone on whom we can dump spiritual truth, we will turn most people off. But if our concern for people is so genuine that sometimes we are not even aware of the transition to verbal witness, people will be drawn like a magnet. Jesus was a "friend of sinners." He was criticized more often for not being separate than for anything else!

He was constantly inviting others to share his daily life. When two of John the Baptist's disciples asked, "Rabbi, where are you staying?" he knew that what they really wanted to know was who he was, not where he spent the night. So he answered, "Come, and you will see." They spent the day with him, and as they got a close-up view of how he lived, they became convinced that he really was the Messiah (John 1: 37-41). He also constantly accepted invitations to share others' lives. Think of his frequent visits to the home of Mary, Martha, and Lazarus, and how often he accepted invitations to eat with Pharisees as well as publicans. Jesus didn't care whether he was host or guest, as long as he could build bridges.

Does that concern for people as they are fill my life? This genuine, open love is the key to sharing. A friend of mine is one of the most aggressive personal evangelists I know. If I tried to witness his way, I would turn people off. But usually he doesn't, because those he speaks to sense he really cares for them.

Bridge building takes both concern and contact. In the various cities where we conduct telephone surveys, we find large portions of the population "unchurched," that is, they do not attend any church at least on a monthly basis. Why? Basically, there are two reasons: (1) they have not met a genuine Christian they would recognize as such, or (2) they do not know a church fellowship that has demonstrated it genuinely cares.

Meaningful contact is the first step in building a bridge to these people. Do as Jesus did: make friendships with non-Christians. You don't have to hunt. Begin with those you contact normally in your neighborhood, business, and social life. Go to games with them. Invite them over for dinner. And if they smoke, have ashtrays available! Otherwise they may assume that becoming a Christian is giving up smoking rather than having a personal trust in Christ.

What if non-Christians invite you to social activities inconsistent with your standards? Decline politely, but don't put the person down by saying, "I don't go to movies like that, I'm a Christian." Instead, suggest something else you might do together.

If Christians want to be the salt of the earth, they must get out of the salt shaker. Salt in the shaker never flavored anything. Furthermore, too much salt in one place tastes terrible and will make you sick! Jesus wants to scatter us as salt throughout the world.

Not long ago I talked with a Christian woman who was trying

to restructure her life in order to make contacts. She went on a tour to Greece with a non-Christian group. She said, "I have my orders. I believe it is possible to go to too many prayer meetings, though not to pray too much. At present, I don't even have permission to go to the missionary circle in my church, although I believe wholeheartedly in missions. But I did get orders from the Lord to join a great-books club." She reported that the discussions were not so profound, but there were no holds barred in discussing her faith with the group.

A church in Vancouver, British Columbia, recently involved its total membership in a study of their priorities and programs. All agreed a top priority was witnessing, but they discovered that most were so involved in church programs they had little time for meaningful contact with non-Christians. For a two-week period, they dropped all programs except for Sunday worship. Instead, the time was used to build bridges in their community. One couple invited neighbors over for dinner. As the guests were leaving, a couple remained behind, saying, "It's been a delightful evening. We've noticed something different about your lives. We'd like to talk with you about it." As a result, they had an opportunity to share Jesus Christ in a very meaningful way.

The common denominators

Another part of bridge building is to discover common interests. We may differ from our non-Christian friends in attitudes, beliefs, and behavior. But if we are going to communicate, we must look for similarities. There is all the difference in the world between perfect God and sinful man. Yet, when God wanted to make contact, he found common ground—"Since the children have flesh and blood, he too shared in their humanity so that by his death he might destroy him who holds the power of death—that is, the devil" (Heb. 2: 14).

Paul's strategy involved stressing points of likeness rather than difference. "To the Jews I became like a Jew, to win the Jews. To those under the law I became like one under the law . . . . To those not having the law I became like one not having the law. . . . To the weak I became weak. . . . I have become all things to all men so that by all possible means I might save some" (1 Cor. 9: 20-22). This was not letting the end justify the means, but letting the end *control* the means. Our ends are a faithful presentation of the gospel and genuine love for others. In seeking common ground, we have no right to be dishonest, to pretend interests that we don't have, to do things against our Christian standards, or to use tactics that make people think we like them, only to drop them if they don't respond.

When Paul went to the intellectual pagan city of Athens, he found a common interest. He began by telling the philosophers he had noticed the images of many gods around the city, especially one erected to "the unknown god." Paul observed that they were very religious, quoted one of their own poets, and then went on to present the story of Jesus and the resurrection.

But the common interest does not have to be religious. Many people feel that Christians are otherworldly creatures who never do anything but read the Bible and go to prayer meetings. Certainly they need to know that God is the hub of our lives. But they also need to know that the rim of our life touches the real world. Do you like tennis? Fishing? Skiing? Then share them with non-Christians. David Spence, a former student at the University of North Carolina, invited friends over for gourmet meals and found that hippies and athletes with nothing else in common enjoyed these dinners. Are you concerned for civil rights, poverty, Christian involvement in politics, or social need? Then become what Francis Schaeffer calls a "cobelligerent" and get involved with some legitimate activities along these lines. Some agnostics and humanists are sincerely interested in other people and believe Christians don't share this interest. You can help to prove them wrong and show that God is concerned in these areas.

Wayne Smith, a Presbyterian missionary in Brazil, felt God calling him to reach government officials in the new capital of Brasilia, a metropolis built in the wilderness. In his spare time, he would go to the government center and meet congressmen, later offering to teach them English. When some of them asked his motive, he frankly admitted two. "I want to be your friend, to know you and your country; teaching you English helps me do this. But I am also here to represent Jesus Christ. If I have the opportunity, I would like to share him with you. If you are not interested, fine—I will teach you English anyway." Out of his witness a Christian fellowship group was formed that had significant influence in that capital.

A further step in bridge building is to look for the good in people. The gospel of Jesus Christ implies that people *need* saving and that people are *worth* saving! God so loved the world that he sent his Son not to condemn it but to save it (John 3: 16, 17).

Jesus Christ looked at the people the way the famous horticulturist Luther Burbank looked at plants. Burbank is said to have viewed every weed as a potential plant.

Take Simon Peter. Others saw a blundering, awkward, unstable fisherman who couldn't be depended on because he was up one moment and down the next. But Jesus changed his name from Simon, meaning "reed," to *Cephas*—Peter—meaning "rock." He knew Peter was weak and unstable, but he also recognized what Peter could be (John 1: 42).

Or think of the woman caught in the act of adultery. Others said she was a worthless sinner and wanted to stone her. But Jesus said, "I know what you are. I don't condemn you, I know what you can be. Go, and sin no more."

Or think of Zacchaeus. Others avoided him because they saw a little, dried-up tax collector who defrauded his people and worked with the Romans. But when Jesus saw him in the tree, he called him by name, recognizing his reputation, but also knowing that he could be a great example of Jesus' power to change people. "Come down immediately. I must stay at your house today," Jesus said (Luke 19: 5).

We Christians stereotype too easily. It is important to link the biblical teaching about people being sinners with the biblical fact that all are made in the image of God, with the potential of being remade.

Wayne Smith, the Brazil missionary, later moved to Atlanta, Georgia, and read that a man there was reputedly the "king of pornographers." Wayne prayed and then went to see him. "I read that you are the king of pornographers," he told the astonished man. "Well, if you've got that kind of ability, you're working for the wrong person. I can imagine what your life could be if God got hold of it." The fellow was so startled by this unorthodox approach that he listened to Wayne and ended up going to church and a Billy Graham crusade!

Stop and think right now: who is the most unlikely person to become a Christian you know? How would Jesus Christ look at that person? What strength do you see in the person's life that Jesus could redeem and use?

A positive attitude of acceptance does not mean we condone everything someone else does. It means that instead of condemning, we seek to communicate an attitude that says, "I love you; I want to be your friend. I can have fun with you, even if I can't go along with everything you do and believe." The older brother in the story of the prodigal son could never have communicated the father's love to his brother. He was so self-righteous, so unconscious of his own need of acceptance and forgiveness that he could only put his brother down.

Our bridge building as Christians also implies long-term availability. During a military operation, the engineer corps may put down a temporary pontoon bridge that can easily be removed. Some of our Christian witnessing may be like that. But in most cases, God wants us to build a permanent bridge that will last. Our attitude must not be, "I'll be your friend if you believe," or "I'll be your friend until you believe," but "I want to be your friend, period." Many times the opportunity to share Christ in-depth does not come until our friendship is tested. But if we are available and vulnerable when a problem comes, if we really help, then the relationship becomes deeper as people say, "You really do care, don't you?"

A big part of bridge building is simply ministering to others in their everyday needs. Today we tend to be skeptical of "do-gooders." There are people who relieve their own frustrations and guilt by helping when they are not wanted. That's not the kind of doing good we need. But it is also recorded that Jesus "went around doing good" (Acts 10:38). Unfortunately, many Christians just go around!

Jesus loved in very concrete ways. He loved with a towel, washing the dirty feet of his disciples and wiping them with a love that served. He also loved with a whip, strange as that may sound. He drove out of the Temple the money changers who ripped off the people by charging them exorbitant prices for sacrificial animals. Most of all, he loved with a cross.

Doing good, showing love, doesn't have to be some heroic action in a major crisis. Often we let the small opportunities pass by—taking a meal to a family when the mother is in the hospital; inviting a new family to share a social occasion; or just dropping by and listening to someone who is depressed.

When I went to Springfield, Illinois, for a crusade, I met a talented masseur named Jim Byron. Because of his own physical problems, he was unable to sit for a long period of time in the meetings. But he offered to give me a rubdown each afternoon as his expression of service. Jim had been a trainer at Wheaton College, and in his off time would give massages to football players to work out their aching muscles.

A freshman once asked, "Why do you do this?"

Simply because as a Christian, he loved the guys, he replied.

"Do you expect me to believe that?" the freshman retorted and insisted he was going to pay.

"If you do, it will be the last time you get a massage," Jim replied. After he left, the guy broke down and admitted to his friends he was bitter because his parents had filed for divorce just before school that fall. Those friends were able to lead him to Christ—and it all started with a love expressed in a practical way through the hands of Jim Byron.

Unfortunately, some churches with a vision for preaching the gospel and doing good overseas seem to miss their immediate neighborhoods. When Roger Fredrikson became pastor of the First Baptist Church of Wichita, Kansas, attendance had fallen off. Besides preaching the Scriptures, Roger shared with the congregation his vision for the church's downtown neighborhood. On a Sunday afternoon, he and sixty members visited the apartments of 180 shut-in, older people. Their message? They simply said three things: God loves you, we care for you, and we would like to help you—is there anything we can do? Most were astounded that they weren't asked to join something, sign something, or give something. These older people needed rides to shop or to the doctor, or someone simply to come and talk. A Wichita newspaper later headlined the story of a church that really cared.

Most bridges are built for two-way traffic, and it's important we learn not only to give but also to receive. We shouldn't act like other people have all the problems and we have all the answers. When Jesus sat down by a hot, dusty well to talk with the Samaritan woman, he began by asking for a drink of water.

If we are hurting, lonely, and down, sometimes the best witness is to admit that we are human, too, and to ask others for their help and understanding.

Our oldest son had a serious physical problem that required precarious open-heart surgery. During this time, we needed a lot of help. We asked Christians to pray. We turned to the doctors for advice. After the crisis was over and Sandy had come back to full health, we heard that one doctor on the case, pretty much of a skeptic, had told his missionary brother that he had been very moved by our family. We were surprised, because many times our grief was obvious and our troubled spirit had shown. But somehow in our weakness and need, this man who had given to us had sensed the presence of the Lord. We were thankful to have been a witness to him out of vulnerability.

1. Helen Shoemaker, *I Stand by the Door* (Waco, Texas: Word, 1969).
2. White, "Witnessing Is Not Brainwashing."

Bridges Are for Traffic

Some years ago a talented Asian student received a scholarship and chose a Christian college in the South. Since she was not a Christian, many students began to pray for her and wonder if she would come to the Lord. When she eventually became a Christian, the girl who influenced her was a rather unknown coed, not one of the campus intellectuals. Asked how this simple girl had led her to Christ, the Chinese girl replied, "She built a bridge from her heart to mine, and Christ walked over it."

Bridges are built not for looks but to bear traffic. And bridge building for Christians is not simply relating to others, but having the kind of relationship that can be a highway for our God.

HOW DO WE MOVE from bridge building to bridge crossing?

I would suggest that the next step in personal communication is to *be an explorer.* When an explorer discovers a new island, he circles until he finds the most likely place to land his boat. A bridge-builder has to explore until he finds the most likely spot to span the water. As communicators, we have to explore patiently the lives of others until we find the route God has opened that offers access to their minds and hearts.

One important way to explore is to listen. This aspect of sharing our faith has been emphasized too little. We habitually think of witnessing as *talking.* We often don't listen sensitively to other people; we simply wait for an opportunity to spout the truth. As a result, the truth we try to communicate does not penetrate deeply into other people's lives.

Some of us are more naturally talkers; others are listeners. But all of us can learn to listen, and even listeners can improve. Though I tend to be more of a listener, I sometimes find my mind wandering instead of listening to another person who is sharing something very important to him. Accordingly, I have worked to focus on not just the words but the feelings behind those words, the "body and soul English" of the person with whom I am conversing.

The next time you are in a social group, notice the people who really pay attention to you. There are some who gaze vacantly off into space or at an imaginary point above your right eye the whole time you are talking. Others only talk to you until someone more important comes along.

A few years ago my wife, some friends, and I visited the headquarters of a certain movement that emphasizes moral renewal. Once the young man we went to see found out who we were, he wasted no time asking about us and our activities. Instead, he launched straight into an indoctrination lecture about their program. My defenses went up. We got out as soon as we could, and I vowed never to unload the gospel on people in that insensitive way.

Unfortunately, we Christians are often as guilty as others. I have visited with leaders of Christian organizations who spent the whole time pumping me full of information about their activities and never asked one question about my ministry or that of others. At times I have been guilty of this too. We need to follow the attitude of Christ Jesus, so that "each of you should look not only to your own interests, but also to the interests of others" (Phil. 2: 4).

Some people listen negatively. As soon as the other person says something they don't agree with, they interrupt and put him right. Other people listen selectively. They hear only what interests or concerns them. The concerned Christian will try to listen sensitively, to understand the other person, to empathize, and to find the open nerve.

Too often, we blow up bridges instead of building them. We need to remember that many people in our world are like

Augustine, playboy of the ancient world who ran off to Rome to find the answer to his perpetual restlessness—and discovered he could find rest only in God.

Jimmy Karam—a businessman, former championship football coach, gambler, and right-hand man to Governor Faubus of Arkansas during the civil rights disturbances of the 1950s—came to speak at a church in our city. Karam had been on the side of those who wanted to keep blacks "in their place." He would hire black people to carry picket signs in order to arouse whites, a tactic he had learned as a strikebreaker.

Then his daughter had asked her pastor to go see him. The pastor had delayed as long as he could. He knew the kind of man Karam was and felt he wouldn't be interested.

When he'd finally gone to his store, he had walked around the block three times before going in and inviting him to church. Jimmy had come the next Sunday. Shortly after that, he'd accepted Jesus Christ, and his life was turned around.

I will never forget how he looked out at the audience and said, "All of my life I have wanted to be like you. I have wanted to be with fine, decent Christian people. But I didn't think I could. I didn't know about the power of God that changed my life. I didn't think you wanted me."

When someone finally explored Jimmy Karam's life, he found an open nerve. As you and I explore the lives of others, we will often find a crisis brewing. There's boredom. There is guilt. There is a deep loneliness. There is a longing for a new kind of life and relationship. As we listen and probe prayerfully, we will recall the one Bible verse or truth that will apply most directly to this person's life.

Be a creative initiator

The next step in personal communication is to *be a creative initiator*. God is! All the way along, God has taken the first step. He made man. He came to talk with man in the garden in the evening. When man sinned, he came calling, "Adam, where are you?" He eventually took the risk of sending his own Son, knowing that in some cases the result would be rejection. If we are going to be like the Father, we need to be creative initiators.

Listening is important, but listening is not enough. Suppose you have a fatal disease and are rescued by a doctor with a miraculous cure. One day you meet someone else with exactly the same symptoms. Would you simply listen and say, "Oh, I'm so sorry"? If so, you would be guilty of inexcusable selfishness. Instead, you would say, "I had that same disease. Let me share the good news of the cure I found."

For many people, the greatest problems in conversing about Christ come at two points: the beginning and the end. We don't know how to introduce faith into our conversation in a natural way, and we don't know how to conclude by actually inviting someone to open his life to Christ.

Why the reluctance? It's partly our natural hesitation to intrude into another person's privacy. Clearly, the God described in Scripture does not want us to batter down doors with various forms of sales persuasion. If someone doesn't want to talk, we can't force him. But at the same time, if we love that person and believe Christ is the answer, we are going to be more concerned about his temporal and eternal well-being than about our embarrassment.

Furthermore, part of this reluctance comes from the opposition of Satan; he doesn't want people to hear the gospel and be saved. We must be aware of his opposition and, with faith in the power of God, take the initiative God is calling us to take.

Let's also realize there are no surefire gimmicks and techniques. Building the bridge of friendship and watching for an opportune time are more important than a dozen fancy methods of witnessing.

However, there are some practical ways we can set the stage to make it easier to take the initiative. Here are a few; you can think of others.

Sharing Christian events

The most obvious approach is to share Christian events with people. Invite others to go to church or Sunday school or some church group with you. It is important to introduce non-Christians to the church so they realize a Christian belongs to a body of people who care for others. Also, the Scripture says, "Faith comes from hearing the message, and the message is heard through the word of Christ" (Rom. 10:17). Exposing people to biblical preaching and teaching will encourage their growth in understanding and faith.

You might start by introducing your friends to a particular Sunday school class or group where they will feel at home. You might suggest that the group plan an evening for each Christian to invite a non-Christian friend. Many people are amazed to find that Christians can have a good time; they end up saying, "I wish there were more things like this. Everybody thinks you have to booze it up to have a good time, but this group disproves that." Of course I am assuming that your group knows how to have fun and how to welcome strangers and make them feel at ease. Wherever possible, an event like this needs to include a well thought-out but low-key presentation of the meaning of Jesus Christ.

Some churches also have "guest" services. Perhaps once a month, the entire program is geared to a presentation of the gospel to outsiders. If your church doesn't have anything like this, suggest it.

Think also of inviting friends to a Christian concert, lecture series, or evangelistic event. During the height of the Watergate crisis, I spoke at the University of Maryland for three days on the subject "Impeach Christ?" Large crowds attended and a number of students came to Christ. A similar series at the University of British Columbia, Canada, on "Anxiety" drew 800 to 900 students a day who had been invited by their friends.

It is unfortunate that some younger Christians have been turned off by mass evangelism because of bad experiences. I still believe this is one basic and effective way God uses. Not long ago I was in San Diego for a Billy Graham crusade. I had breakfast with a writer, an active young Christian who is nevertheless turned off by most traditional Christian events. The night before, he had taken some non-Christian neighbors to the crusade. He took them skeptically because he had been trying to relate to them for several years, and they were just not interested. Instead of being negative on the way home, they plied him with question after question about Christianity. Obviously, the thousands of people who were there impressed them, and the simple straightforward message broke through a crust of indifference and brought them a new sense of awareness that this fellow could follow through.

I must confess that I wouldn't take some of my friends to just any evangelistic event. I would be sure a clear presentation of the gospel was going to be made, emphasizing basic Christianity without getting into side issues. What Paul called the "offense of the cross" (Gal. 5: 11) is unavoidable, but the presentation itself doesn't have to be offensive. Furthermore, I would want to be sure any closing invitation would be given in an honest way, without guile, manipulation, or undue emotional pressure.

When we take our friends to these events, we need to follow through. After the meeting I would say, "Well, what did you think of that tonight? What were your impressions?" I would ask if they had any questions. Eventually I might ask, "Have you ever thought of committing your life to Jesus Christ? Or are you still on the way?" This shows them I am prepared for negative answers and will not jump down their throats if they say no.

Sharing Christian friends

Some fascinating Christians from the United States and over-seas come to visit in our home. From time to time, we invite neighbors or friends to meet these individuals. After light re-freshments, we ask them to tell who they are, where they are from, what their work for the Lord involves, and some interest-ing things they see happening. Conversation can be started in a very low-key, non-threatening way.

The guest doesn't have to be a celebrity. An ordinary Chris-tian friend of yours who may have something exciting and genuine to share about Christ can open the subject. Be sure your guest of honor understands what you are doing and is prepared to speak. It's also important to let your friends know ahead of time what to expect. Be honest with them. Don't invite them to a concert or to meet a friend under false pretenses.

Sharing literature

You can give books and articles to people. If you have read something in a Christian magazine about an issue that is impor-tant to a non-Christian friend—abortion, homosexuality, sin-gleness, money, husband-wife relationships, divorce, rearing children—pass it on. Say to your friend, "Here's an article I thought you might like to see. When you're through I'd be interested in knowing your thoughts."

If your friend is interested in politics, look for some of the fine books by Christian politicians. Charles Colson's *Born Again* has been a tremendous eye-opener for some. If someone is concerned about race relations, try Eldridge Cleaver's account of turning from the Black Panther Party to his current commitment to Jesus Christ.

Michael Green, an English writer, has written books such as *Man Alive* and *Runaway World* that give a lucid presentation of Christianity and are easily read. Billy Graham's best-sellers *Peace with God* and *How to Be Born Again* have influenced millions. A wealthy Swiss financier was given a copy of one of Billy's books but tossed it down when he saw it was religious. One night he could not sleep; he looked for something to read and came across that book. After reading the first chapter, he thought to himself, *This is an intelligent man; he knows what's going on in the world.* He read all night and six weeks later told his startled family that he was no longer an atheist but believed in Jesus Christ. (That man's son later married Billy Graham's daughter!)

To someone who is grieving over the loss of a loved one, you might give Joseph Bayly's book, *Heaven.* I am thankful that today more and more books are written by Christians who are women, who are scientists, who are blacks, and who skillfully interpret the gospel from their standpoints.

Sharing the Scripture

Bible discussion groups are one of the most effective settings to introduce Christianity to those who might not attend a formal church service. These small groups can be held in college dorms, homes, and even in businesses. For several years my wife has taught a weekly class of young mothers. Many who have come are either anti-religious or too "sophisticated," because of their college studies, to take the Bible seriously. Some are almost totally ignorant of the Bible's contents. In an atmosphere of open, intelligent, and practical discussion of the Bible and how it relates to their lives, many of these young mothers have moved to a genuine faith.

When you invite non-Christians to such a group, think how you would feel if you were coming for the first time. Try to put these visitors at ease. Have extra Bibles in a modern translation on hand. Don't expect them to know where Obadiah and Ecclesiastes are located. Give the page number. Remember, many people aren't familiar with our Christian jargon or short-hand terms for the different versions—"RSV," "King James," or "Amplified"—and discussions about their relative merits are absolutely foreign.

Invite questions, and if you don't know the answer, admit it and say you will find out. Keep the discussion based more on what the Bible says than on opinions of what it says. Remember, it is exposure to the Word of God in the context of love, concern, and faith that helps change attitudes.

Sharing at work

Look for opportunities in your vocational field to share your faith. A friend of mine who is a professor of psychiatry at a major university was asked to edit a standard textbook in his field for the university press. He was able to assign certain chapters on subjects such as guilt and death to himself and some Christian colleagues so they could write from the framework of their faith.

Dr. Charles Dunn, head of the political science department at Clemson University, chose "My Last Lecture" as his topic for an awards convocation speech. He spelled out explicitly that if this were his last lecture, he would want people to understand fully the values he found in being a Christian. His conclusion: "I don't say you have to believe what I do, but this is what I believe. If this were your last lecture, what would you say?"

Of course the major witness we make on the job has to be by demonstration. Unfortunately, many Christians never realize work is a major stewardship. Sloppiness and slipshod attitudes toward work only bring ridicule on words we say about the gospel. Christians in a certain Eastern European country were asked why they worked so hard. "Well," they replied, "we are not allowed to initiate a conversation about Jesus Christ in our country. But we can work hard and show that we are motivated people by our disciplined lives. When we are asked why, then we can explain it is because of Jesus Christ in us."

As we minister to the needs of those around us on the job, loving our neighbor-worker as ourselves, opportunities to share Christ will often emerge.

Mary Crowley of Dallas has 14,000 employees working in her franchise operation. When one of her representatives gets behind in her payments, Mary Crowley doesn't send a curt letter. She phones the person, often finding there is illness or a family problem. Then she may fly there to offer help and advice. Sometimes she even says, "You need the money more than we do, so just forget what you owe us this month." Invariably those people turn out to be her best representatives. They also gain a new respect for Mary's Christian commitment.

In Rome, Georgia, I met William Sanders, a black bellman in a Holiday Inn. When he saw a Bible in my hand, he asked if I were a Christian and said he was too. He said that men often think he can get them liquor or a girl. When they insist, he points to the open Bible in the motel room and says, "Why don't you try reading that book? That's where you will find what you're looking for."

One day he had to deliver some beer to the room of a man who had been drinking several days. He asked for some more liquor. Sanders showed him the Bible instead and said, "Jesus can give you what you want." The man invited him in, and they ended up on their knees in prayer. The next morning the man was sober. "William," he said, "I am going back home. You have shown me something I needed."

Sharing through social contacts

Don't overlook your social contacts. A young Christian I know has a real gift in photography. He has put together some impressive slide presentations accompanied by well-chosen Christian music that speak of the love, reality, and personal nature of the Lord of all creation. He and his wife invite friends from their apartment complex for a social evening and use these slide presentations to introduce conversation about their faith.

A businessman I met in Dallas is a real tennis nut. He and his wife started inviting some of their tennis partners over for dinner, two or three couples at a time. After dinner they go into the living room, and he says something like this: "You know, at the tennis club it seems like we only know one another's first names and how we serve and lob. I thought it might be interesting to get to know each other on a little deeper level. How about each of us sharing the priorities in our lives?" Then he usually tells something of his background, his work, and his interests, ending with "The priorities in my life are first, my relationship with Jesus Christ; second, my family; third, my job."

Then his wife will often say something similar. There is no pressure beyond that point, but they continue around the room asking everyone to talk about what is important to them. In almost every case, someone will come up either later that evening or on a subsequent occasion and say, "What did you mean when you said that Jesus Christ was the most important thing in your life?"

Sharing through social groups

Look for positive and creative ways to introduce Christian fellowship to your different associations. In the city where we live, one of our friends was concerned to bring a witness to her Junior League crowd. She suggested a Christmas brunch to think about the real meaning of the Christmas season. They finally agreed to invite a woman from Alabama, an ex-alcoholic whom Christ had set free. She described coming out of a stupor one Christmas and praying the one-word prayer "Help!" She told how "Jesus Christ was born again in the dirty stable of my heart." It made headlines in our paper. This resulted in a Bible class being started for many of these women in our city and eventually led to an area-wide conference on creative living that drew several hundred people.

Sharing through conversation

One of the most important initiatives we can take is to follow God's guidance in our conversations. It is always interesting to overhear a nearby table in a restaurant and realize how superficial the talk is. Yet many people are willing to talk deeply about things, provided they can do so with someone who will use a normal tone of voice and not embarrass them. Billy Graham is a master at introducing Christian things into a conversation through what I call the oblique approach. We might be sitting at a table with some people, and Billy will say, "Last week I was talking with a man about this same thing. We got into an interesting conversation, and this is what I said to him . . . ." He then lets the rest of us "listen in" on a conversation he had with someone else. This way we get the message without feeling he is preaching.

If you have had an interesting experience at a Christian meeting or have been reading something provocative, bring it into your conversation. We talk about other things we have been doing; why not talk naturally and honestly about the Christian part of our lives?

Watch for current topics that can provide a starting point. For example, "I read the other day in a Gallup Poll that 34 percent of American adults say they have had an experience of being born again. That's interesting, because I've had that experience, but I didn't think the number would be that high. Have you ever had that experience, or have you ever met anyone else who had?"

Questions can be a very useful stimulus to conversation. A student who traveled through Europe one summer asked those he got into more than casual conversation with, "What do you think is wrong with the world?" Almost invariably the answer would boil down to selfishness. He would go on and ask, "What is your major goal in life?" And just as often the answer would seem to be, "Happiness—for myself"! This contrast fueled a number of significant conversations.

Sometime ago I found a series of questions that I find helpful in certain circumstances.

Question 1: "Are you interested in spiritual things?" Or more specifically, "Are you interested in Christianity?"

If the answer is yes, the second question is, "Have you ever thought about becoming a *real* Christian?"

However, if the first answer is no, and the person seems open, the second question can become, "Have you *ever* considered becoming a real Christian?"

Whether the second answer is yes or no, you can go on to the third question: "If someone asked you to define a real Christian, what would you say?" This oblique approach introduces a hypothetical third person and removes some of the tension of direct confrontation. It also tells you this person's relationship to Christ and how clearly he understands the essence of Christianity.

In some situations, I would feel free to use a sequence of questions such as this. However, such an approach must never be seen simply as a technique or gimmick. It should never be substituted for sensitivity to a person and should not be used to trick or goad someone who is not interested.

Techniques and subtle approaches may be helpful. But it is

more important to develop the ability to get inside people and understand them. On a recent flight I sat across the aisle from the dean of a private prep school. He asked me what I did, and I emphasized not my role as an evangelist but my trying to communicate how Jesus Christ relates to people's lives.

He wanted to talk more. I found out he was an agnostic with a high sense of moral and ethical ideals. Furthermore, he was a seeker. Because his academic subject was English, I began to talk about the English author C. S. Lewis. This fellow loved the outdoors, so I related Lewis's experience as an atheist. Frequently in his life he was "surprised by joy," sudden flashes of delight and pleasure. He began to ask where this joy came from and how it could be explained. This adventure led him to believe in God and Jesus Christ.

The dean then told me about a friend of his, another teacher who is a hedonist, one who makes pleasure the end of life. He rationalized his guilt by saying, "I'm getting my kicks exploiting them, but they're getting their kicks exploiting me. I'm doing them some good, and they're doing me some good."

"I can't buy that," the dean said. "As I see it, we don't have to exploit people. We can explore another personality, but that doesn't have to involve exploitation."

"I'm with you," I replied. "But based on your beliefs, your friend may be right. If there is no God, why not exploit people?

"But if there is an infinite Creator God, then we can realize that we are creatures with needs to fulfill. Since we are made with personalities in the image of God, we don't have to exploit, as an animal might exploit another animal."

His face lit up. He said, "That gives me another perspective on this whole thing."

He was not ready to make a commitment to Jesus Christ, but exploring the possibility of a God who was really there was the starting point in communicating with him.

There is no set pattern for personal communication. Instead, we have to grow in the art of communication, in understanding our faith, and in knowing and exploring other people. We have to grow in terms of trusting God. We have to demonstrate his reality in our lives; our faith must be visible. And we have to look creatively, patiently, and expectantly for the openings that help us to be storytellers for God.

II

Tell Me the Old, New Story

Joe Bayly, author of the well-known satire, The Gospel Blimp, *has written another equally poignant but less-known parable entitled "I Saw Gooley Fly." Herb Gooley, as Bayly describes him, was a college student, "an ordinary sort of guy until the night he stepped out of his third-floor dorm window and flew away into the wild blue yonder."*

Up until Christmas break his junior year, Gooley had been distinguished by only one thing—the knack of tripping over his own feet. But when he got back from Christmas vacation, his astonished fellow students found he was actually able to fly— fly his own body, that is, not an airplane.

His roommate told how it happened. After studying late one night, Gooley decided to go down the street for a hamburger. His roommate reminded him that the hamburger place would close in just three minutes, to which Gooley replied matter-of-factly, "I'll fly down."

He went over to the window, lifted it up, and stepped out. Jerry, his roommate, thought he had gone crazy and ran around telling everybody that Gooley had jumped out the window. But when they looked outside, no one was there.

The whole campus buzzed. They would see Gooley walking along, and all of a sudden he would be airborne. The library was besieged with requests for books on aerodynamics and anything else that had to do with flying. Everyone wanted to learn to fly like Gooley, but nobody would actually admit to envy. The administration was embarrassed by this flight freak, so they invited a specialist to give lectures for a "Flight Emphasis Week." The hall was packed until the students found out the lecturer couldn't fly. The crowd suddenly dropped off.

The parable ends as follows:

"You know, I've always been surprised that Gooley didn't tell us how to do it, or at least how he did it. He couldn't help knowing how interested we all were. But he kept his mouth shut. So none of us learned to fly.

"It's a funny thing, but I still have a sense of loss at not learning Gooley's secret. And other grads have confessed the same thing to me.

"What happened to Gooley? I've often wondered about that. He transferred that fall to another college where, they say, all the students know how to fly." [1]

But in your hearts acknowledge Christ as the holy Lord. Always be prepared to give an answer to everyone who asks you to give the reason for the hope that you have.

—1 Peter 3:15

IT TAKES WORDS to get the gospel across. The early part of the Book of Acts shows how demonstration leads to conversation. In Acts 2 the early church was together, the Holy Spirit filled them, and they began speaking about Jesus with great joy using strange tongues. People thought they were drunk. But Peter explained that this was a fulfillment of God's promise in the Old Testament, brought to reality in Jesus Christ.

In Acts 3 we read that Peter and John told a lame man to walk in the name of Jesus. The people were astonished, and Peter said, "Why do you stare at us as if by our own power or godliness we had made this man walk? The God of Abraham, Isaac and Jacob, the God of our fathers, has glorified his servant Jesus" (Acts 3:12, 13). He went on to tell the story of Christ.

When I say it takes words, I don't necessarily mean speechmaking. If you don't have gifts as a public speaker, you can still talk about Christ in ordinary conversation.

Telling his story

Witnessing for Christ primarily means being a storyteller. Christ stimulated people by telling parables. When religious leaders accused him of consorting with "sinners," Jesus didn't answer with a long discourse on hamartiology (which, believe it or not, means "theology of sin"!). Instead he told three simple, profound stories about a lost sheep, a lost coin, and a lost son.

The leaders saw sin as "badness," but Jesus portrayed sin in these stories as "awayness"—being away from God as the sheep was from the fold, the coin from the purse, and the son from the father's home. In each case Jesus drew further probing from the people who were interested, involving them in a two-way communication. At the same time, people with "closed filters" weeded themselves out of the process, because they weren't ready to hear more. Jesus' storytelling approach is a good guide for us.

Theologian David Hubbard makes the point that

> the Jesus People movement, the most dynamic para-church organizations, and the congregations and denominations which charted the greatest growth have been those which have seemed to have stuck more closely to the simple story of the gospel and have not trimmed the high demands which Christian discipleship places upon those who would follow Jesus.

He goes on to note that

> God knew what He was doing when He told the most significant things about Himself, not in proverbs, nor in sonnets, nor in chronological lists, nor in theological propositions, but in a story.[2]

Most Bible scholars agree that the early Christians' message contained two basic parts—first, an announcement of what God had done through Jesus Christ for our salvation; secondly, an invitation for us to receive this salvation. The exact points they emphasized depended upon their hearers and their situation.

Michael Green imagines Peter telling the story of the woman with the hemorrhage.

> Look at her state. This flow of blood was only a little thing, but a serious one. It cut her off from her family, her synagogue and thus from her God. . . . It gradually weakened her whole constitution as it went on year after year. And, worst of all, it was, humanly speaking, incurable. Is that not the situation you are in? Your sins may not seem large in your eyes, yet they separate you from your family, your fellows, and your God. They increasingly grip your life. . . . They, humanly speaking, are incurable. Then listen to what I have to tell you. This woman had heard about Jesus; she came up behind Jesus in a crowd, she touched Jesus by faith . . . and at once she was healed. . . . If Jesus can do it for her, He can do it for you.[3]

The next time you read through the Gospels, think of the miraculous healings in that light. There is no one way to tell the story of Jesus Christ. John, in selecting material for his Gospel, was guided by this principle: "These are written that you may believe that Jesus is the Christ, the Son of God, and that by believing you may have life in his name" (John 20:31). In a similar way, we have to select the points that will help others to believe. If we are witnessing to someone who feels that religion will save him, we might use the story of Nicodemus, to whom Jesus said, "You must be born again." If someone holds to material things as God, we tell him about the rich young ruler. A person torn apart by psychological or moral conflicts might relate to the man who called himself "Legion" because he was tormented by an army of evil spirits until Jesus liberated him.

What about "canned" techniques?

I personally believe that preplanned approaches have their place, but we have to weigh both their value and dangers.

Most people need some practical handles by which to share

their faith. When I was at a summer camp in my early teens, someone presented to me the so-called Roman Road to salvation. This consists of selected verses having to do with man's sin (Rom. 3:23), Christ's provision—salvation by his death (Rom. 5:8), and our receiving God's free gift (Rom. 6:23). I can remember writing this sequence into the margins of my Bible, noting the next verse by the previous one. I would never have begun witnessing, gained confidence, and learned other ways of approaching people if I hadn't had some way to begin.

Another value of such techniques is that they present the gospel fairly systematically. They move from God's creative purpose, to man's sin, to God's provision in Jesus Christ, to the response we need to make.

But they also have dangers and limitations.

First, no technique is going to work with everyone. Evangelism is more than a sales technique. And even the best sales techniques don't always work! I know of a young insurance man who went to a motivational seminar. The speaker explained that life insurance salesmen are really philanthropists—they create great sums of money to be used for those in need. He related that whenever he sits next to someone in an airplane, he asks the person what he does. The person replies and then asks what the salesman does, thereby setting up his reply, "I alleviate hunger, fear, and poverty." The person usually asks if he is a doctor, and he replies, "No, I'm a philanthropist," and then goes on to explain life insurance.

The young man thought this was a great idea. So flying home from the seminar, he asked his unsuspecting seatmate what his work was. The man told him—and stopped. No follow-up question. The first part of the surefire approach had broken down!

The stewardess passed out some cookies, and the young man decided to give them to his seatmate. At this point, he resumed the conversation and said, "By the way, what do you do?"

"I alleviate hunger, fear, and poverty."

"Are you a doctor?"

"No, I'm a philanthropist."

The man looked at him with a blank stare and said, "Well, thanks for the cookies," and turned away!

A deeper danger is that an overemphasis on techniques may depersonalize our witnessing. Unfortunately, much "personal evangelism" is impersonal. It is concerned with getting across a preprogrammed "plan of salvation" instead of the Person. If we are going to be like Jesus, we ought to treat others as persons, not cases.

A programmed style of presenting our faith may help eliminate the unknown and give us a feeling of control. But that which takes away the fear often takes away the excitement of witnessing. The line of patter that never varies can easily go stale. Not that the gospel message can be altered, but the way we present it ought to be flexible.

Ford Madison, one of the most effective lay witnesses I know, told me about a fellow worker—whom we will call Steve—who was an outright pagan. Meeting Steve for the first time in several months, Ford learned that he had become a committed Christian because of an incident that had occurred between them. One day Ford had asked Steve what was the most important word in his vocabulary.

Quick as a flash, Steve had shot back, "Profit."

Ford had replied, "That's interesting. Did you know the Bible talks about profit? It says that 'all scripture is given by inspiration of God, and is *profitable* for doctrine, for reproof, for correction, for instruction in righteousness' " (2 Tim. 3: 16, KJV). Ford hadn't given the conversation a second thought.

But Steve had. He'd decided that if there was profit in the Bible, he wanted to learn about it. So he'd begun to read the Bible, had come to know the power of the gospel, and had accepted Christ.

Ford commented, "Who would ever have thought of using that particular verse, which is clearly directed to believers, as a means of witnessing!"

But perhaps the greatest danger in using techniques is that we may come to trust in the technique instead of in God. Paul expressed his distrust of any human method when he wrote to the Christians at Corinth, "I came to you in weakness and fear, and with much trembling. My message and my preaching were not with wise and persuasive words, but with a demonstration of the Spirit's power, so that your faith might not rest on men's wisdom, but on God's power" (1 Cor. 2: 3-5).

Any technique or method not regarded as only a tool soon becomes an idol.

Genuine communication is a three-way conversation among God, ourselves, and the person with whom we are sharing. In this conversation, techniques can have a useful purpose, provided we recognize their dangers and limitations. Everyone should have some method of presenting the gospel systematically and clearly, and it is better to have several to choose from. But being able to devise a presentation that suits the situation is best of all. Witnessing is like fishing. We can catch a fish with a bare hook—my youngest son once caught one that way. But the more equipment we have and the more we understand the fish, the better fishermen we will be.

What are the basics?

What is the minimum truth a person needs to know to become a Christian? It is hazardous to answer that question, because the Bible doesn't give us a "minimum package." However, the essential truths of the Christian message are:

1. God's purpose
2. Man's need
3. Christ's provision
4. Man's response

Here are some basic statements about these truths and some ways they are expressed in Scripture.

1. God's purpose

   God, who created all things, loves you and has a destiny for your life.

   "So God created man in his own image, in the image of God he created him; male and female he created them" (Gen. 1: 27).

   "From one man he made every nation of men, that they should inhabit the whole earth; and he determined the times set for them and the exact places where they should live. God did this so that men would seek him and perhaps reach out for him and find him, though he is not far from each one of us" (Acts 17: 26, 27).

God is just and holy; that is, he punishes all evil and expels it from his presence.

"The wrath of God is being revealed from heaven against all the godlessness and wickedness of men who suppress the truth by their wickedness" (Rom. 1: 18).

2. Man's need

God made us for himself to find our purpose and fulfillment in fellowship with him.

"For by him all things were created: things in heaven and on earth, visible and invisible, whether thrones or powers or rulers or authorities; all things were created by him and for him" (Col. 1: 16).

But all human beings have rebelled and turned away from God.

"All we like sheep have gone astray; we have turned every one to his own way" (Isa. 53: 6).

This results in separation from God.

"Your iniquities have made a separation between you and your God, and your sins have hid his face from you so that he does not hear" (Isa. 59: 2).

The penalty is eternal death.

"For the wages of sin is death, but the gift of God is eternal life through Christ Jesus our Lord" (Rom. 6: 23).

3. Christ's provision

In spite of our rebellion, God kept on loving us. He became man in the person of Jesus Christ to restore our broken relationship.

"For God was pleased to have all his fullness dwell in him, and through him to reconcile to himself all things" (Col. 1: 19, 20).

Jesus Christ died for us in order to pay the death penalty for our rebellion.

"But God demonstrates his own love for us in this: While we were still sinners, Christ died for us" (Rom. 5: 8).

"For Christ died for your sins once for all, the righteous

for the unrighteous, to bring you to God. He was put to death in the body but made alive by the Spirit" (1 Pet. 3: 18).

He came back to life from the dead. He is alive today to give a new life and fellowship with God to those who believe.

"The thief comes only to steal and kill and destroy; I have come that they may have life, and have it to the full" (John 10: 10).

4. Man's Response

God commands me to recognize and confess my condition before God as a sinner.

"For all have sinned and fall short of the glory of God" (Rom. 3: 23).

"If we confess our sins, he is faithful and just and will forgive us our sins and purify us from all unrighteousness" (1 John 1: 9).

God commands me to repent, that is, to turn from my sins to serve him as Lord.

"From that time on Jesus began to preach, 'Repent, for the kingdom of heaven is near' " (Matt. 4: 17).

God commands me to trust Jesus Christ as my Savior and be willing to follow him as Lord.

"If you confess with your mouth, 'Jesus is Lord,' and believe in your heart that God raised him from the dead, you will be saved" (Rom. 10: 9).

"Yet to all who received him, to those who believed in his name, he gave the right to become children of God" (John 1: 12).

How to present the basics

A number of helpful tools have been developed to communicate these basic truths.

THE ROMAN ROAD

Man's sin: "For all have sinned and fall short of the glory of God" (Rom. 3: 23).

Sin's Penalty: "For the wages of sin is death, but the gift of God is eternal life through Jesus Christ our Lord" (Rom. 6: 23).

God's provision: "But God demonstrates his own love for us in this: While we were still sinners, Christ died for us" (Rom. 5: 8).

Man's response of faith: "That if you confess with your mouth, 'Jesus is Lord,' and believe in your heart that God raised him from the dead, you will be saved" (Rom. 10: 9).

Man's response of commitment: "Therefore, I urge you, brothers, in view of God's mercy, to offer yourselves as living sacrifices, holy and pleasing to God—which is your spiritual worship. Do not conform any longer to the pattern of this world, but be transformed by the renewing of your mind. Then you will be able to test and approve what God's will is—his good, pleasing and perfect will" (Rom. 12: 1, 2).

My only reservation in using the Roman Road is that I would prefer to start with God's creative love and purpose before moving to man's sin.

THE GOSPEL OF JOHN

Since John's Gospel was purposely written to communicate faith to non-Christians, many Christian communicators like to use its passages. It is so profound that great scholars have never completely mined its depths, yet so simple that nuggets of truth lie on the surface, as it were, for a child to pick up.

God's purpose: "In the beginning was the Word, and the Word was with God, and the Word was God. He was with God in the beginning. Through him all things were made; without him nothing was made that has been made" (John 1: 1-3).

Man's need: "In reply Jesus declared, 'I tell you the truth, unless a man is born again, he cannot see the kingdom of God' " (John 3: 3).

God's provision: "The Word became flesh, and lived for a while among us. We have seen his glory, the glory of the one and only Son, who came from the Father, full of grace and truth" (John 1: 14).

"For God so loved the world that he gave his one and only Son, that whoever believes in him shall not perish but have everlasting life" (John 3: 16).

In all of life there is nothing more wonderful
than discovering peace with God.

STEP 1 TO THIS DISCOVERY IS REALIZING
GOD'S PLAN . . .
PEACE AND LIFE

GOD LOVES YOU AND WANTS YOU TO EXPERIENCE
PEACE AND LIFE —— ABUNDANT AND ETERNAL.

"...I am come that they might have life, and that they might
have it more abundantly."
John 10:10

Since God planned for us to have peace, and the abundant life
right now, why are most people not having this experience?

STEP 2 IS ACKNOWLEDGING
MAN'S PROBLEM . . .
SEPARATION

God created man in HIS own image and gave him an abundant
life. He did not make him as a robot to automatically love and
obey Him, but gave him a will and freedom of choice.

MAN chose to disobey God and go
his own willful way. Man still
makes this choice today. This
results in SEPARATION from God.

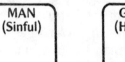

"For all have sinned, and come short of the glory of God."
Romans 3:23

Man through the ages has tried to
bridge this gap in many ways...
without success. ...

There is only one remedy for this
problem of separation.

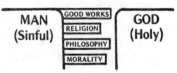

STEP 3 IS RECOGNIZING GOD'S REMEDY... THE CROSS

"JESUS CHRIST is the ONLY answer to this problem of separation. When Jesus Christ died on the Cross and rose from the grave, He paid the penalty for our sin and bridged the gap from God to man. HIS DEATH and RESURRECTION make a new life possible for all who believe."

MAN (Sinful) | **CHRIST** | **GOD (Holy)**

"God is on one side and all the people on the other side, and Christ Jesus, Himself man, is between them to bring them together."

1 Timothy 2:5, The Living Bible

"Jesus saith unto him, I am the way, the truth, and the life: no man cometh unto the Father, but by me."   John 14:6

God has provided the ONLY way...Man must make the choice...

STEP 4 IS MAN'S RESPONSE... RECEIVE CHRIST

We must TRUST JESUS CHRIST and RECEIVE HIM by personal invitation.

The BIBLE says...
"Behold, I stand at the door, and knock (Christ is speaking): if any man hear my voice, and open the door, I will come in to him."

Revelation 3:20

Are you here..........or here?

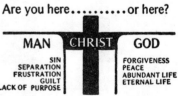

MAN | CHRIST | GOD
SIN / SEPARATION / FRUSTRATION / GUILT / LACK OF PURPOSE | | FORGIVENESS / PEACE / ABUNDANT LIFE / ETERNAL LIFE

IS THERE ANY GOOD REASON WHY YOU CANNOT RECEIVE JESUS CHRIST RIGHT NOW?

What you must do:

1. Admit your need (I am a sinner).
2. Be willing to turn from your sins (repent).
3. Believe that Jesus Christ died for you on the Cross and rose from the grave.
4. Through prayer, invite Jesus Christ to come in and control your life. (Receive Him as Savior and Lord.)

Man's response: "Yet to all who received him, to those who
    believed in his name, he gave the right to become children
    of God" (John 1:12).

"Whoever puts his faith in the Son has eternal life, but
    whoever rejects the Son will not see that life, for God's
    wrath remains on him" (John 3:36).

STEPS TO PEACE WITH GOD

This little booklet (reproduced on pages 138-39) was designed by the Billy Graham Evangelistic Association for crusade
counselors. It is also helpful in personal conversation.

It incorporates the widely used illustration of the bridge—the
gap sin has made, man's futile efforts to close it, and the link
Jesus Christ has made from God's side to ours. Such a diagram
helps people grasp the concept. Even without the booklet, I
have often drawn the bridge diagram on a napkin or the nearest
piece of paper for someone, letting him read the Scriptures
directly from the Bible. Almost invariably he asks to take the
diagram with him.

OTHER VISUAL TOOLS

In Kenneth Smith's book, *Learning to Be a Man,* he gives the
following time line and suggests that it be used to answer man's
four basic questions:

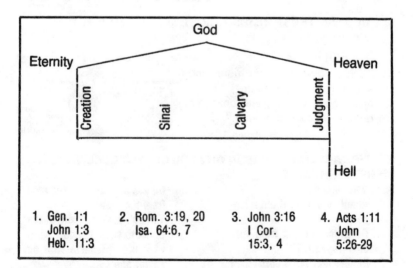

1. "Who am I?"—a creature made by God with value and purpose.

2. "What am I like?"—frustrated and anxious because of spiritual rebellion.

3. "What do I need?"—Jesus Christ's death to bear the penalty for my sins.

4. "What is going to happen to me?"—I am moving either toward heaven or hell.[4]

This then leads logically to a fifth question: "What will I do about God's sacrifice, about God's provision in Jesus Christ?"

Ron Rand designed the "Three Circles of Christianity" after several years of frustration over how best to share with people in a brief encounter. This presentation can be made in less than a minute or expanded over a longer period of time. It can be mounted on both sides of a 3″ x 5″ card, as shown on page 142, or drawn as you talk.

The Scriptures previously mentioned can be used in explaining the first three circles. The three *you's* are also quite obvious. The first *you* (with a cross in the center *O*) is the person who has received Jesus Christ into the center of his life. The second *you* (with the cross at the bottom of the *O*) symbolizes a person who has received Christ but has put him at the side of his life. The third *you* (the empty *O*) indicates someone who has never received Christ.

Developing your own approach

Once you have grasped the basic truths we have outlined and surveyed different approaches, try putting the gospel into your own words. One way is to picture a real or imaginary friend who is not a Christian. Then sit down and write a letter to that person, trying to explain the gospel message simply and intelligently.

Ask a Christian friend to read what you've written and give reactions. Then, give it to a non-Christian and say, "I have been trying to express what my Christian faith means to me in words that people can understand. I would really appreciate your reading this and telling me if I have gotten my point across and if anything is unclear.

Once you have the basics fixed in your mind, it is time to express them verbally. Again, start with a sympathetic Christian friend. Either adopt one of the approaches outlined above or

SIDE 1

3 CIRCLES OF CHRISTIANITY

☺ GOD LOVES YOU

☹ GOD HATES SIN

⊕ GOD SENT JESUS

WHICH OF THESE 3 ARE

YOU⊕

YOU⊕

YOU⊕

JESUS said, "Behold, I stand at the door and knock; if anyone hears my voice and OPENS the door, I WILL COME IN TO HIM." Rev. 3:20

JESUS, I DESIRE to be changed. I OPEN my heart to you and ASK you to come in and forgive me. AMEN.

SIDE 2

RECEIVED

The moment that YOU ☺ RECEIVED

Jesus Christ many things happened, including the following:

S SINS forgiven I John 1:9
SPIRIT received Holy Spirit Gals. 4:6

M MEMBER of God's family John 1:12

I IN you—Christ now lives   Rev. 3:20
                                Gals. 2:20

L LOVE — God loves YOU John 3:16
LIFE
1. new — II Cor. 5:17
2. abundant — John 10:10
3. eternal — 1 John 5:11-13, John 3:16
4. book of — name written in Rev. 3:5

E ETERNAL security or salvation
                               John 10:28

NOW <u>THAT'S</u> SOMETHING TO ☺ ABOUT!

devise one of your own. Soon you are ready to plunge in prayerfully and expectantly with someone who does not know the Lord.

To summarize the steps to effective verbal witnessing, go through this checklist:

☐ I have reviewed the gospel basics.

☐ I have memorized key Scriptures and/or their references.

☐ I have written the message in my own words.

☐ I have practiced presenting it to a Christian friend.

☐ I am ready to try it with a non-Christian.

☐ I have made an actual presentation!

Learn to tell your story

Not only did the first Christians tell Jesus' story, they also told their own stories. Paul related his story of meeting Jesus on the road to Damascus on at least two occasions (Acts 22, 26). Knowing that personal evidence cannot easily be dismissed, Peter and John said, "We cannot help speaking about what we have seen and heard" (Acts 4: 20). Personal testimony was a powerful tool in their lives.

It is true that the early Christians never advanced their experience as the reason others ought to believe. Neither should we ask others to base their faith merely on our experiences with Christ. If I say to someone, "Jesus Christ has given me life, joy, peace, and purpose," he can come back with "Meditation has done the same for me." We have to point outside our own experiences to the historical facts of Jesus Christ's life, death, and resurrection.

Still, while our experience is not the basis of our faith, it is a validation of that faith. Jesus' life and resurrection is the foundation; Jesus in my life today is the superstructure. Sharing Jesus Christ means first to tell his story and then to tell my story.

The ability to tell our own Christian pilgrimage honestly, directly, and convincingly is tremendously important. People who are unmoved by the theoretical often identify with the personal. Many times I have noticed Billy Graham struggling to get a point across, when suddenly he just stops preaching and begins to relate how as a boy of seventeen he came to know Jesus Christ. Almost always a hush seems to fall over the audience.

The personal testimony has a built-in authority. Nobody could argue with the blind man who said, "Whether or not he is a sinner, I don't know. I do know one thing: I was blind but now I can see" (John 9:25).

Each of us has a story that is worth sharing, because everyone is important to God, and every person's life has been planned by God.

As a young Christian, it used to bother me that I didn't have any earthshaking experience like Paul. I hadn't mainlined heroin or knifed anybody in a gang fight. So I tended to feel that God had shortchanged me, and that I would be much more effective if I had a dramatic story to tell. Then one day I realized that most people don't have some cataclysmic turning point in their lives. In fact, I could identify far more with the average person because I *didn't* have a spectacular story to tell.

I think every Christian should think through his own story so he can present it effectively in about ninety seconds.

If you read through the testimonies of Paul in Acts (for example, chapter 22), you will find he basically told what his life was like before he came to Christ, how he came to meet Jesus Christ, and what happened after.

Try using that form yourself. Think through and write your story based on this outline:

1. Your life and attitudes before you came to follow Christ.

2. How you came to realize your need for him.

3. How you came to know Christ.

4. What has happened since—what Jesus Christ means in your life today.

If, like myself, you came to know Christ at an early age, you may find it difficult to put your testimony into that outline. I was glad to read Ron Rand's suggested approach for those who became Christians at an early age:

1. Tell about your home life, your early Christian experience, and people who influenced you as a child.

2. Explain your early understanding of what it means to be a Christian.

3. Describe how you came to relate personally to Jesus as your Lord and Savior.

4. Tell some specific areas in your life that Christ has changed and others where you still need him to make changes.

How to use your testimony

Let God lead you. Don't feel you have to give your testimony every time. Be sensitive and let the Holy Spirit tell you when the time is right.

Make it personal. Don't try to mimic the exciting experiences or profound explanations someone else uses.

Keep it honest. You don't need to embellish your story or make it more glamorous. In fact, it is good to write it down so you won't keep adding to it in years to come! The more you keep your story the way it really happened, the more it will ring true.

Keep it up-to-date. A layman asked, "What has Jesus Christ meant to you since seven this morning?"

Make it understandable. Give plenty of personal details. People identify with the little touches that make your story vivid and human. And use language people can identify with.

Contrast these two:

Approach 1: "I was saved when I was a teenager and have lived a happy Christian life ever since."

Approach 2: "The summer when I was fourteen, I was having a hard time. My parents were on the verge of breaking up. I was terribly lonely. Then I met a group of kids who were really turned-on Christians. There was something about the way they sang and the way they loved me. They took me to a meeting where I heard a man tell about the possibility of a personal relationship to Christ. I really wanted this, but I was bothered. I can remember going out into the night, looking up at the stars, and saying, 'Jesus Christ, I don't know if you are really there, but if you are I want you to come into my life.' "

Don't be bound to "total replay." Try to emphasize the part of your experience that matches where the person is struggling now. If I were talking to someone who believed in Christ but didn't have assurance, I would tell them of how as a boy of nine I prayed and said, "Jesus Christ, I think I have received you, but if I haven't, I want to do it now," and how that underlined what I already believed. If someone were having an intellectual struggle with the Bible, I might tell about some of the doubts I had in college days and how I came to find a firm foundation for my faith in historic Christianity. On the other hand, if the person were going through a family problem, I might share how when our oldest son was fourteen he had a very serious problem that required open-heart surgery and how God ministered to our family at that time.

Be sure to concentrate more on who God is and what Christ has done than on your sin or experience. I have heard some people tell the sordid part of their lives in such a way that people got a vicarious thrill out of this person's sins rather than identifying with the power of Christ. I have also heard people tell their salvation experience in such glowing terms that all the attention was on themselves and not the Savior. So tell your story humbly.

Finally, have a hook. At the end of your testimony, don't just let it drop, but ask, "Have you found this peace with God?" or "Have you ever experienced this thing of being born again?" or "Have you established a personal relationship with Jesus Christ?" Depending on what else you may have shared, this can lead into the presentation of the gospel basics or directly to an invitation to accept Christ.

1. Joseph Bayly, *How Silently, How Silently (and Other Stories)* (Elgin, Ill.: David C. Cook, 1968), p. 27.
2. David Hubbard, "Understanding the Gospel" (unpublished paper), p. 9.
3. Green, *Evangelism in the Early Church*, p. 64.
4. Kenneth Smith, *Learning to Be a Man* (Downers Grove, Ill.: InterVarsity, 1970).

12

King James,
Ken Taylor, and You

"I could believe in Jesus Christ, if it weren't for my barber," the man had said to me.

A barber? Between him and Christ? Didn't add up, so I asked for details. The barber lived next door; he was a good barber—clean, fast, cheap and always gave a free sermon instead of green stamps.

The man gave me the following account:

Take last week for example, I walk in the shop, hang up my hat and put on my most friendly voice: "Hi, what's new?"

"Nothing," the barber replies, "except the good news that Christ died to save sinners and that sure includes you."

"That's new? You've been playing that line to me for ten years. Like a stuck record."

"Yeah, well, the only thing new would be if you'd listen to it for a change," says the barber, then adds, " 'Beware lest thou forget the Lord.' "

"You can forget it as far as I'm concerned," I tell 'im and try to start a conversation—oh—on the weather, politics, anything.

But the barber just keeps clobbering me with what must be stuff from the Bible: " 'We must all give an account before the judgment seat of

Christ'—'The wicked shall be turned into hell'—
'How will you escape if you neglect so great salva-
tion?' "

Well, he got through to me all right so I say,
"Look, if you care so much about my soul, where
were you when I was in the hospital last month?"

"Well, I was busy," the barber answers. "You
know how my work keeps me tied down here."

"Yeah—you were busy chasing the almighty
dollar, that's what, if I know you. And I almost
died—but did you come to talk to me? Huh-uh—
you didn't care."

"Care? Of course I care. Why I've warned you
over and over. The Bible says, 'It is appointed unto
man once to die and after that—the judgment,' "
he replies, stropping away with his razor. . . .[1]

—David Augsburger

YOU, A BIBLE TRANSLATOR?

You're not exactly a seventeenth-century scholar turning out
beautiful cadences of rich Elizabethan language . . . or a Wycliffe
missionary spending twenty years in a remote Indian village,
analyzing the sounds and finally putting God's own Word in the
language of the tribe . . . or even Ken Taylor, frustrated enough
by the *thee's* and *thou's* as he read the Bible to his children that
he painstakingly paraphrased it into everyday American English
as he rode the commuter train to Chicago, finally producing the
famous Living Bible.

But you are a Bible translator. *All* Christian communication is
a matter of translation. When missionaries go overseas, they
spend large sums for language school and cross-cultural study.
Yet "at home" how many of us take the trouble to learn the
vocabulary and thought forms of our non-Christian neighbors
around the corner?

Jesus saves—at the First National Bank?

What do you think of first when you hear the word *saved?* "It's
what I wish I'd done with my last paycheck" was a popular reply
when Wheaton College communications students surveyed

passersby at a local shopping center. The word *redemption* often brought to mind green stamps.

"If we want to build meaning, we have to start where people are," says Richard Senzig, the professor who directed the survey. "Christians must not insist that people come to us. Jesus went to the people with words they could understand." Senzig had mixed reactions when the words *born again* appeared in bold type on the cover of *Newsweek.* He was initially pleased, but then he was struck by the responsibility the exposure implied. "Here's the whole world looking at this phrase," he said, "and I am responsible to interpret it to my neighbor who is not a Christian."

If a non-Christian turns down my sharing of the good news, I have to ask myself, "Did he understand the message and not want it? Or didn't he understand?" As we go on in the Christian life, we tend to develop an insider's vocabulary. Our terminology includes "saved," "lost," "blessed," and the need to "repent," "be born again," and "have a personal relationship with God." Outsiders may comprehend little if anything of the meaning.

Biblical metaphors are sometimes even more obscure without explanation. "Are you clothed in righteousness?" a well-meaning person asked the non-Christian sister of a young man I know. She stared at him in blank bewilderment. It is not that there is anything wrong with any of these words or truths. The task is to explain, illustrate, and translate them so that people understand.

Dr. Eugene Nida, a leading scholar in Bible translation, explains that to translate means to give "the closest equivalent, first in meaning and secondly in style." Asked which is the best modern translation of the Scripture, Nida says, "The one which communicates the truth most effectively to the constituency in question."[2] We need to get our message across in a form that will communicate its meaning and in a style that will be understood.

The first translators

"When studying the approach of Christians to Jews and Gentiles, rich and poor, clever and unintelligent, over the first two centuries, I was amazed at the variety in their proclamation," says Michael Green.[3] Jesus was a Jew, and the first communication of the good news was to the Jewish people, so translation wasn't much of a problem at the beginning.

"But on Gentile soil, it was different," notes Green. "The first evangelists engaged in extensive translation work not so much of words as of concepts. They did not begin by quoting Old Testament texts; they started from the felt needs of the hearers and used imagery that would communicate with them."[4]

In Athens, Paul found a point of contact with the pagan philosophers in the altar "to the unknown god" he had seen as he walked about the city.

When he wrote to the Romans, he talked about "adoption." This was a concept that pagans knew well but was foreign to the Jewish culture.

In talking to the Jews about the death of Jesus, Paul emphasized the question "How can we be right with God?" Guilt and forgiveness were tremendously important to these people, who had been taught about the one God and his commandments. But Gentiles did not have this same teaching, so Paul portrayed Jesus Christ as the liberator who by his death sets people free from bondage (see, for example, Col. 2:15). This made sense to pagans obsessed with demonic powers and fates that controlled their lives.

Look at how John begins his Gospel with the *logos,* which to thinking Gentiles meant the universal Reason, the eternal order of reality that lies behind everything good in this world. In John 1:14 he writes, "The Word [*logos*] became flesh and lived for a while among us." Here is the one place, he says, where reality has broken through into our human order!

A Christian named Clement in Rome even used the mythical phoenix bird, which is depicted as rising from the ashes of destruction, as a picture of the Resurrection. These first Christians were not afraid to use risky translations, determined as Paul was to "become all things to all men that by all possible means I might save some" (1 Cor. 9:22).

Their aim was not to soft-pedal the hard parts of the gospel but to present it in understandable cultural forms. Of course, they made mistakes. Sometimes they were so intent on reaching the Gentiles that they not only removed the Jewish wrappings but also lost some of the content of the package. But as

Green concludes, "If Christ is for all men, then evangelists must run the risk of being misunderstood, of misunderstanding elements in the Gospel themselves, of losing out on the transposition of parts of the message so long as they bear witness to him. Christians are called to live dangerously. The principle of the incarnation must be carried into Christian preaching."[5]

Speaking to needs

A crucial question to ask as we translate the gospel for our friends is how close we are to their needs.

Jane meets a non-Christian named Mary at the PTA. Before really getting to know her, Jane asks, "Mary, would you like to know how to have a full and meaningful life?" Mary seems indifferent and unresponsive.

As they part, Jane thinks to herself, *Well, I guess she's just not interested in spiritual things.*

But Mary says to herself, *I wish she would help me know how to face the fact that my doctor says I have less than six months to live.*

Certainly the Lord could use the question about a full and meaningful life. But if Jane had taken the trouble to get to know Mary, the gap between her presentation and Mary's need would have been much smaller, and she would have had a much better opportunity to communicate.

If you talk to a teenager about heaven, he might be more concerned about his rotten home life. It is not that death does not concern him, but we have to find the point where God is currently working in the life of this individual.

Don Richardson, missionary author, believes God has put parallels or analogies in the traditions and ideas of every culture, into which the gospel can be meaningfully introduced. He tells of a primitive Pacific tribe where the communication gap seemed so huge that it could not be bridged. Then, by observation, a missionary found the point of contact. Two families of this tribe had been feuding. The feud could be ended only by a symbolic ritual in which the members of the hostile clans lined up opposite each other in the shape of a womb. Representatives from each side then walked through the symbolic womb together, and when they emerged at the other end, peace was declared. It didn't take much imagination for the missionaries to use this as an illustration of how through the "new birth" people can come to peace with God and with each other.

As you and I witness to friends in our own culture, we have to go through the same process. Listening sensitively to their words, thoughts, fears, and hopes will often show us the divinely ordered point of contact in their lives.

At this point, however, we have to be very careful. It is possible that in using these points of contact to translate the gospel we actually could lose the heart of the gospel. Dr. Nida, for example, emphasizes that a point of contact with a non-Christian is not necessarily common ground. For example, both Christians and Muslims believe that God reveals his truth. But for the Muslim, God sends his truth without ever coming personally. In Christianity, the heart of the matter is God personally coming in Jesus Christ.

Many Christians today are very impressed with what is called "relational theology." They suggest that we approach people on the basis of their psychological felt needs. Some rely heavily on the so-called hierarchy of values of psychologist Abraham Maslow. Maslow has suggested that all human beings have certain common needs arranged in an ascending order.

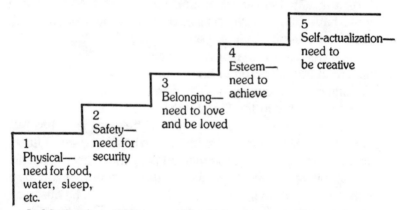

In Maslow's opinion, most North Americans today are at step 3—they have a particular need to belong. He is probably right. Physical needs and security needs have basically been satisfied. Therefore, an experience of Christian fellowship that meets the need to belong may well be one of the first things that draws people to Christ.

But precisely here is the danger. If we say to the non-

Christian, "We all sense a need of belonging," he will agree. If we say that Christian fellowship is a good way to experience belonging, he may also agree. But he is *not* agreeing with the message of the Bible. He is merely saying that Christianity is useful, not that it is true.

So in translating the gospel, we may begin with man's need for belonging. But we must also show that the reason for loneliness and estrangement is that we are "separate from Christ... without hope and without God in the world." And we must explain that through Jesus Christ those who are far away can be "brought near through the blood of Christ" and become a member of the new family of God (see Eph. 2:12, 13, 18).

Treasure in jars of clay

Next comes the very style in which we communicate. We have a supernatural message, but we don't need a supernatural tone of voice or a superspiritual gaze on our faces. Paul reminds us that "we have this treasure [the gospel] in jars of clay to show that this all-surpassing power is from God and not from us" (2 Cor. 4:7). We may be speaking for God, but we don't need a reverberation unit!

It reminds me of the little boy who was playing in the yard and found a rat. He stomped it to death and then ran into the house holding it by the tail to show his mother. The pastor had just stopped by to visit. The little guy came in shouting, "Mommy, mommy, mommy! Look what I found! I kicked it and stomped it and kicked it and stomped it—" when suddenly he saw the pastor sitting there. He saw his mother about to go into shock. So quickly he changed his voice and solemnly intoned, "—and the Lord called him home"!

A newspaper story about a Jesus commune noted that its members do not discuss politics, sports, or world and local events, because Jesus was all they felt they needed. But the real Jesus is related to all of life. He talked about heaven and hell and his Father with utter seriousness, but he also talked about money, fishing, weddings, and sex. His first miracle was at a wedding party, where he supplied the wine. He lived with such gusto that his enemies mistakenly condemned him as "a glutton and a drunkard" (Luke 7:34).

Of course, the other extreme can be even more offensive. I

have heard Christians use suggestive language or throw in an occasional cuss word to show that they are still "one of the guys." That has the stench of hypocrisy just as much as the person who puts on a superpious pose; it disgusts genuine people, whether they are Christians or not. "Worldier than thou" is no better than "holier than thou."

The effective translators are those whose life-style reflects a God who is just as present in the maintenance shop as in the chapel, who do and say everything for him, and who know that he is not obsessed with religion but is the God of every part of their lives.

New wine in new wineskins

The fact that some people—perhaps many—do not understand words like *sin, faith,* and *repentance* is no reason to give them up. As Christians, we believe God directed the writers of the Bible to use the words they did to convey God's exact message. "All Scripture is God-breathed" (2 Tim. 3:16). Yet God gave the words of Scripture in the common languages of the day. When Paul gave his testimony before King Agrippa, he made a point of saying that on the road to Damascus he had heard Jesus Christ speaking to him *in Aramaic* (Acts 26:14). Our God speaks Yiddish, Chinese, British English, American English, and all the tongues of the human race. And part of the exciting task of sharing our faith is to help translate his direct words into the language of our friends. Here are a few practical suggestions as to how to do it:

1. Use a modern translation or paraphrase of the Bible. I love the majestic language of the King James Version. Its beauty may never be surpassed. We all need to study and learn it for its great heritage. But God is not tied to seventeenth-century English, eighteenth-century architecture, nineteenth-century hymns, and twentieth-century cliches. An up-to-date translation can make a truth much more understandable to someone who has not read the Scripture. Compare these two versions of Romans 3:20:

King James: "Therefore by the deeds of the law there shall no flesh be justified in his sight: for by the law is the knowledge of sin."

Good News Bible: "For no one is put right in God's sight by doing what the Law requires; what the Law does is to make man know that he has sinned."

2. Take key words in the presentation of the gospel, and think of synonyms or phrases that will explain them.

For example:

Eternal life—"a fifth dimension of living" or "God's kind of life"

Believe in the Lord Jesus Christ—"put your trust in the Lord Jesus Christ"

Saved—"rescued" or "set free"

Redemption—"liberation, like a slave being set free"

Sin—"not just what I do but what I am—being away from God"

Image of God—"being created so I can personally know God and show who he is"

Hell—"where we'll exist in the state of eternal separation from God"

Try using different words of Scripture to say the same thing. For example, *kingdom of God, eternal life,* and *saved* are all interchangeable in the New Testament. The disciples talked about the kingdom of God to Jews but used words such as *salvation* and *eternal life* with Gentiles who didn't identify with the kingdom concept.

Never be afraid to use the words of Scripture. God's Word is more important than ours. But do interpret, and keep your mind open to the Holy Spirit to make the truth plain.

3. Borrow illustrations, or come up with your own. Be looking constantly for analogies from your life and the lives of people you meet. Jesus often used analogies and parables to lead people from what they knew to what they didn't know.

Again, a few contemporary illustrations:

A Christian teacher was explaining eternal life to his non-Christian principal. He drew two dots and connected them with a line. "That is what I think you mean by life," he said. "It begins at birth and ends at death." Then he put down two more dots and drew a line that started slightly ahead of the first and ran beyond the second. "That is what I mean by eternal life," he explained. "Christians believe life begins at conception and goes on into eternity. Birth and death are events along the way."

The idea of God becoming man is, of course, hard to grasp. Only the Holy Spirit can make this plain. When Peter said to Jesus, "You are the Christ, the Son of the living God," Jesus replied, "This was not revealed to you by man, but by my Father in heaven" (Matt. 16:16, 17). But we can illustrate it. One of the best stories for this purpose is the boy who was crazy about bugs. One of his favorite pastimes was to go out in the backyard and listen to his radio while watching ants build an anthill. One day he heard on the radio that the anteater had escaped from the zoo a couple of blocks away. He became frantic. He tried to warn the ants of their danger. But they didn't pay any attention to him. He was too big, and they were too small.

He thought to himself, *If only I could become an ant like they are, then I could warn them of the danger.* Of course, he couldn't. But God, who created everything, could become man so that he could identify with us and warn us of the danger of sin. That is what he did in Jesus Christ.

To many people the word *saved* speaks of either a negative or an emotional experience. I like to use this illustration: Suppose I were drowning, and you jumped in and pulled me out, rescued me and applied artificial respiration. When I came back to consciousness, I would say, "You saved me." What would I mean? That you had done for me what I couldn't do for myself. I owe my life to you. *Saved* does not necessarily mean walking the church aisle or having some emotional experience. It describes God coming to rescue us from our self-centeredness, setting us free to serve him and others.

Redemption is a wonderful word. In the Bible it describes a slave saving up enough money to buy his freedom or someone else purchasing freedom for him. So Jesus Christ paid the redemption price—himself—to set us free from the bondage of our self-will.

A Nashville banker gave me a great illustration of this. When he was a boy, his older brother told him, "You're my slave—I bought you from mama for a dollar." The younger brother believed him! Every time his brother told him to do something, he felt he had to obey. If he had a piece of pie and his brother wanted it, he had to give it up. After several months, he went to his mother one day in tears and told her he didn't want to be his brother's slave anymore. She was amazed and didn't know what he was talking about, so he explained how his brother had bought him.

His mother was very wise. She didn't laugh or try to talk him out of his mistaken idea. She just went to her purse, got a dollar, gave it to his brother, and told him she had bought him back and he didn't have to be his brother's slave anymore.

To many non-Christians *faith* is a word for people who are not smart enough to reason out the truth. A little boy once said, "Faith is believing what you know isn't true." We need to let people know that faith is not belief without evidence, but commitment without reservation. "Scientific proof" does not apply to relationships between persons. If I am sick, for example, you may say, "Dr. Williams is a specialist in this area." You may tell me about his training, his experience, his reputation, and the cases in which he has succeeded in treating this disease over the years. But I will never know whether this is really true until I act on the evidence and actually put myself into his hands. That is when I exercise faith. Without faith, I can never really know if he is a good doctor.

Faith is taking the evidence from history, from the lives of other people, from the claims of Jesus Christ himself, and then committing myself to him.

These few examples show how we can try to translate into terms and analogies people can understand.

Models of Jesus Christ

Important as language is, translation is more than an exercise in words. Translation is a total involvement, and the heart of translation is Jesus Christ being modeled in our lives. "In this world we are like him," wrote the apostle John (1 John 4:17).

It is not enough to say, "Jesus is the answer." We have to be willing to say, "Jesus, *be* the answer through me." As God wrapped his love in the personality of Jesus two millennia ago, so he wants to wrap his love in us today.

Eugene Nida tells of talking to one of the great missionary pioneers of Guatemala. Well into his sixties, the man was setting out on another of his walking visits to Indian congregations in small mountain villages.

I asked him why he did not drive his car in view of his increasingly poor health (he often took sick on such trips) and the new route that had just come through that region, for he could have driven to many of the places he proposed to visit. His reply was simple. "Oh, I never drive, for the people I want to reach are not used to someone driving up in a car. What is more, I never found a man that I could not speak to about Jesus Christ if only we were walking down the same road.[6]

God could have put his message for mankind in flaming letters of lightning across the sky. He could have had it sung by angels for the whole world to hear. Instead, he translated himself into his Son, who walked the hot, dusty roads of Palestine. Today, again, God could translate his message into all the thousands of cultures and languages by running it through some gigantic computer. But he has chosen not to do so. He still chooses to communicate his truth through human personalities. He chooses to walk narrow paths of tropical jungles, hard sidewalks of concrete jungles, and grassy lawns of suburban jungles through translators like you and me, if we will take the risk of letting his treasure be carried to a lost and seeking world in the clay jars of our imperfect lives.

1. David Augsburger, *Are They Getting the Message?* (Chicago: Moody, 1968), pp. 3-5.
2. Eugene A. Nida, *Message and Mission* (New York: Harper & Row, 1960), pp. 194, 205.
3. *Let the Earth Hear His Voice,* p. 162.
4. *Let the Earth Hear His Voice,* p. 162.
5. Green, *Evangelism in the Early Church,* p. 142.
6. Nida, *Message and Mission,* p. 229.

13

The Reasons Why

It is not more spiritual to believe without asking questions. It is not more Biblical. It is less Biblical and eventually it will be less spiritual because the whole man will not be involved.

Consider the ministry of our Lord Jesus himself. He was a man who constantly answered questions. But someone will say, "Didn't He say that to be saved you have to be a little child?" Of course, He did. But did you ever see a little child who didn't ask questions? . . .

Christianity demands that we have enough compassion to learn the questions of our generation.[1]

—Francis Schaeffer

AS SOON AS WE SET OUT to share our faith, we discover we are not on a one-way street. Witnessing is dialogue, not monologue. It includes listening to other people, understanding their objections, fears, and questions, and seeking seriously to give solid answers.

Let's be clear that no one but God himself has all the answers. Some things we know; others we don't. We must not be afraid to say, "I don't know the answer, but I'll be glad to try to find out." A little genuine humility would help matters greatly.

Some Christians get very defensive when questions are raised about the faith. They take it as a sure indicator of unbelief. True, some questions can be an intellectual smokescreen for an unwillingness to let God be God. On the other hand, people do have genuine questions that must be faced.

Faith in Jesus Christ is not a leap in the dark. In the Scriptures it is called "obeying the truth" several times. God has not made us mindless. Jesus said that we are to love God with all our mind as well as with all our heart. The psalmist tells us not to be "like a horse or a mule, without understanding" (32: 8). God said through Isaiah the prophet, "Come now, let us reason together" (1: 18). Jesus Christ frequently entered into debate and dialogue. Notice also the words used in Acts to describe the witnessing of the early Christians. They "taught," "argued," "disputed," "confounded," "proved," and "confuted powerfully."

A person may respond at least temporarily to the gospel through personal influence or emotional persuasion. But if we don't deal with his intellectual problems, sooner or later he may fall away.

The Bible teaches two complementary truths about the mind. The first is that God has made our minds and deals with us as his reasonable creatures. The other side is that "the god of this age has blinded the minds of unbelievers, so that they cannot see the light of the gospel of the glory of Christ, who is the image of God" (2 Cor. 4: 4).

It is often said that the basic problem in evangelism is communication, that people don't believe because they don't understand the gospel. But there is a deeper problem. Men have been blinded by the god of this world. In Romans 1, Paul tells us that man has sufficient knowledge to enter into a relationship with God, but he suppresses that truth. Sin distorts the intellect at the level of the will.

Richard Halverson, pastor of Fourth Presbyterian Church in Washington, D.C., was leading an evangelistic discussion at a college fraternity some years ago. One student asked him, "Can you prove that Jesus Christ ever lived?"

Halverson answered with a question of his own, "Do you believe that George Washington was the first President of the United States?"

The student was clever enough to realize that he was caught in a trap of his own making. If he said yes, he would have to admit he believed in Washington on historical evidence. Then he would have to face evidence for Jesus Christ's historical reality. So he grinned, said, "No, I don't believe that," and disappeared out the doorway! He wasn't looking for answers, just a reason to bolster his unbelief.

When God converts a whole person—heart, mind, soul, and will—he does not bypass the intellect. He illuminates the intellect through the Holy Spirit. God may use a verse of Scripture, a simple testimony, or an intellectual answer to put the light of Christ into someone's life. I like the way John Stott, the well-known English preacher, sums up our responsibility: "We cannot pander to a man's intellectual arrogance, but we must cater to his intellectual integrity."

At the same time, a human being is more than a mind. The respect given to intellectuals in our day has sometimes led us to overemphasize the rational. A college campus, for example, can be a rarefied atmosphere where the cerebral is almost worshiped out of proportion. Furthermore, Christians have sometimes divorced Scripture's emphasis on truth and doctrine from its equal emphasis on the relational aspects of our lives. Even intellectuals don't spend all their time meditating on philosophical problems. They cry, laugh, make love, get disappointed, are jealous, and are afraid to die just like anybody else. Fred Smith, a prize-winning biochemist at the University of Minnesota, was once invited to hear Billy Graham preach at a Youth for Christ rally. He went with disdain to hear a message he knew would be beneath his intellectual level. But the need of a new birth somehow gripped him. For three days he could hardly sleep or eat as he realized he had standards for his academic life but none by which to measure his personal life. He gave his life to Christ and was a strong and vibrant witness at the university until his death.

Many times intellectual problems are related to very personal experiences. Some years ago when I was speaking at a private school in Canada, a girl kept plying me with questions about how I could believe in a personal God. She ridiculed the "simplistic" idea of a "father" who could care for us. I found that theology was not the root of the problem at all. Her father had deserted and divorced her mother when this girl was in her early teens. She was still so bitter that she lashed out, rejecting the very idea of a God who could care.

Bigger commitments, bigger questions

The more important a decision is, the more questions I am likely to ask. If I'm shopping for a mousetrap, I'm not likely to spend an hour quizzing the store owner about how it works. But I remember well when my wife and I bought our first house. It was not a snap decision. We spent several weeks coming to the conclusion that we really did need to buy our own house. Then we began shopping around until we found one that would meet our needs and desires—three bedrooms, a den with a fireplace, a porch, and a quiet street without too much traffic.

When we finally found such a house, we checked it out carefully. We researched the reputation of the builder and what guarantees we would have against major defects. Finally, we had to sit down and calculate the cost against our limited income.

When we invite someone to Christ, we are asking him to make the ultimate once-in-an-eternal-lifetime commitment. We should be glad, not dismayed, if he has some genuine questions. Commitment to Jesus Christ involves at a deeper level all of the questions my wife and I faced as we considered buying a house:

1. Do I need Christianity?
2. Does it really meet my needs?
3. What guarantees do I have that I can rely on Jesus Christ?
4. Am I willing to make the commitment at the cost involved?

In the appendix of this book I have listed a number of the serious questions non-Christians ask. I have also suggested ways we can respond. It is helpful to think through such exchanges in advance so that we can guide people through the decision-making process.

All the preliminary questions, of course, eventually lead to the most crucial one of all: "Am I willing to make the commitment Christ asks?"

More than a few people come right to this brink of decision—and then draw back. How should we handle hesitation?

There was both tenderness and toughness in the way Jesus dealt with uncertainty. If someone had honest doubts and problems, he was very patient. When Thomas expressed his disbelief in the Resurrection, Jesus appeared to him. He didn't scold him; he simply extended his hands and said, "Thomas, look at the evidence. See the nail prints. Decide for yourself." But when he met people who refused his call to discipleship for no good reason, he could be very direct and uncompromising. Once when he said to a man, "Follow me," the man replied, "Lord, first let me go and bury my father." This was probably a vernacular way of saying, "I've got to wait until my father dies and I've finished my family responsibilities. Then I'll think about God's kingdom."

But Jesus said, "Let the dead bury their own dead, but you go and proclaim the kingdom of God" (Luke 9:59, 60).

Yet Jesus would never force anybody. When a rich young ruler turned away from his call, Jesus didn't run after him and try to make him come back. Still, he was filled with compassion. He wept over the city which had largely rejected him and his message: "O Jerusalem, Jerusalem, you who kill the prophets and stone those sent to you, how often I have longed to gather your children together, as a hen gathers her chicks under her wings, but you were not willing" (Matt. 23:37).

We need to be as realistic as Jesus was. If we present the gospel, and there is no positive response, we often feel guilty. "If only I had presented the message more clearly," or "If I had been more filled with the Spirit," or "If I had been more loving." But even Jesus met indifference and unbelief.

We may find some people, as Jesus did, who say, "I want to believe, but help my unbelief." They hesitate because they just do not understand enough. What they need is time and love and patience. We need to encourage and help them to study the Scriptures, to deal with their objections and problems, and to stay with them until they are ready.

We will find others who say, "I'm afraid." During meetings at the University of Georgia, I spoke with a coed about opening the door of her life to the knock of Christ. "I'm afraid he won't be there," she said. In the past she had been let down, and she was afraid God would do the same.

Others will be afraid that God is going to take something good out of their lives. To such people I think we need to underline Jesus' promise: "The thief comes only to steal and kill and destroy; I have come that they may have life, and have it to the full" (John 10:10). The only things Christ takes away are the things that will destroy and mar our lives and separate us from God eternally. Everything good and beautiful he will make better and more abundant. .

Some are afraid of themselves. "I'm just not strong enough. I am afraid I can't hold out." We need to help them to realize that God is not expecting them to sprout self-grown angel's wings. God asks us to come to him just as we are. 1 Corinthians 10: 13 reassures us, "No temptation has seized you except what is common to man. And God is faithful; he will not let you be tempted beyond what you can bear. But when you are tempted, he will provide a way out so that you can stand up under it."

Still others hesitate because they are afraid of what others will think. They need to be encouraged to realize (a) they can be a positive influence on others, and (b) Jesus said, "If anyone is ashamed of me and my words . . . the Son of Man will be ashamed of him when he comes in his Father's glory" (Mark 8: 38). We can't be private Christians. We must be open about it. At the same time, our friends need to know that they will have new Christian brothers and sisters who will stand with them and encourage them.

Sometimes it helps those who are hesitant to take one very specific first step of commitment. On the road to Damascus, God didn't tell Paul he was going to write a major chunk of the New Testament, be whipped, beaten, and persecuted, and start churches all through the Mediterranean area! If he had, Paul might have dug a foxhole beside the road and stayed there. All the Lord said was, "Get up and go into the city, and you will be told what you must do" (Acts 9: 6). We can help people take such a first step, to pray, "Lord, I give as much as I know of myself right now to as much as I know of you right now."

It's like walking down a dark road with a flashlight. You have a mile to go, but your flashlight only shows thirty feet. Do you refuse to start out because you can see only thirty feet? Of course not. We are asking people to commit themselves to Jesus Christ for a lifetime. But they begin where they are, at that specific point, to commit the next "thirty feet" to him, trusting him for the future.

What if the answer is no?

There will always be those who hold back, not out of fear or a lack of understanding, but for no good reason or because they are unwilling to let God be God in their lives. When Jesus faced this kind of refusal, he never pressured anybody, but at the same time he made the issue clear and warned that the refusal of God's invitation meant judgment.

In the preface of *The Great Divorce,* his parable on heaven and hell, C. S. Lewis writes,

> You can't take all luggage with you on all journeys; on one journey even your right hand and your right eye may be among the things you have to leave behind. We are not living in a world where all roads are radii of a circle and where all, if followed long enough, will therefore draw gradually nearer and finally meet at the center. Rather in a world where every road, after a few miles, forks into two, and each of those into two again, and at each fork you must make a decision. . . . I do not think that all who choose wrong roads perish; but their rescue consists in being put back on the right road. A wrong sum can be put right: But only by going back until you find the error and working afresh from that point, never simply by *going on.* . . . If we insist on keeping Hell we shall not see Heaven: If we accept Heaven we shall not be able to retain even the smallest and most intimate souvenirs of Hell.[2]

Lewis is reflecting the rigorous words of Jesus Christ. People who like to say, "My religion is the Sermon on the Mount," might be surprised if they actually read some of its parts:

> "If your right eye causes you to sin, gouge it out and throw it away. It is better for you to lose one part of your body than for your whole body to be thrown into hell" (Matt. 5:29).

> "Wide is the gate and broad is the road that leads to destruction, and many enter through it. But small is the gate and narrow the road that leads to life, and only a few find it" (Matt. 7:13, 14).

> "Not everyone who says to me, 'Lord, Lord,' will enter the kingdom of heaven, but only he who does the will of my Father who is in heaven" (Matt. 7:21).

Not to decide is to decide. Delay carried to its ultimate end is the same as rejection. With deep compassion and concern we must let our friends know that God's word is *today* and the devil's word is *tomorrow*. "Do not boast about tomorrow, for you do not know what a day may bring forth" (Prov. 27: 1). "Now is the time of God's favor, now is the day of salvation" (2 Cor. 6: 2).

Delay is foolish, because we have no guarantee of future opportunity. A rabbi in ancient times had a stock answer for the question "When shall we repent?"

"Repent the day before you die," he always advised.

"But we don't know when we will die," people would say.

"Then repent today."

Furthermore, delay is selfish. Many of us want to wait until we have done everything we want, until we have fulfilled all our other obligations, and then we will give the worn-out ends of our lives to God. Is that kind of commitment worthy of a God who gave his all for us?

Great sensitivity is needed at this point. Before we present someone with this kind of warning, we need to be very sure that he understands the gospel clearly, that he has had time to think through the issues, and that we have helped him face his fears, objections, and honest problems. When we are sure that someone is deliberately delaying or refusing, a warning about the consequences is in order.

Even then, we must make it clear that our friendship, concern, and love will not stop. For some non-Christians, this is the most important test of whether their Christian friends really love them. "If I don't accept Christ, will you drop me? Are you interested only in my spiritual scalp?" God loves us with an *everlasting* love. Even at the final Day of Judgment, when people will go to hell, I believe Jesus Christ will be saying, "I still love them. How many times I wanted them to come, but they wouldn't do it." If God loves like that, so must we.

George Mueller, a nineteenth-century British Christian, was well-known as a man of faith and prayer. Once he picked out five friends whom he wanted to see become Christians. He began to pray for them. Within about five years, two of them accepted Christ. Twenty years later, one more came. He kept on praying for the other two daily for nearly forty years until he died. Both of those men became Christians within two years after Mueller's death!

To sum up, honest and intelligent answers to honest and seeking questions are an important part of sharing our faith. A deep desire to persuade others is not only right but crucial. "Since, then, we know what it is to fear the Lord, we try to persuade men," wrote Paul in 2 Cor. 5:11. Manipulation, however, is always wrong. Paul also said, "We have denounced secret and shameful ways; we do not use deception, nor do we distort the word of God. On the contrary, by setting forth the truth plainly we commend ourselves to every man's conscience in the sight of God" (2 Cor. 4:2). While we seek to persuade, we always remember that God the Holy Spirit is the Hidden Persuader.

1. Paul E. Little, ed., *Reaching All* (Minneapolis: World Wide, 1974), p. 139.
2. C. S. Lewis, *The Great Divorce* (New York: Macmillan, 1946), pp. 5-6.

14

How to
Be an Introducer

The day Eldridge Cleaver, author of Soul on Ice
*and former Black Panther, was set free on bond, I
spent 2½ hours listening to his journey from Marx-
ism to Christ.*

*His quest was not openly religious; it was rather
a search for meaning and purpose, for the source
of his own creativity. He could find none of these
in the materialism of his Marxist philosophy.*

*Finally, while living in exile in France, he came
to the verge of suicide. One night he looked up at
the moon and began to see visions—his own face,
former heroes such as Mao Tse-tung and Che
Guevara, and finally the face of Jesus Christ. That
experience caused him to return to the United
States and surrender to authorities.*

*In a federal holding center in San Diego, a local
black minister came to visit him. Cleaver recounted the story of his search and the vision he
had seen. The pastor then said, "Eldridge, you
have seen Jesus in the moon. I want you to meet
Jesus Christ in the Bible." Holding his Bible and
turning to an empty chair, he said, "Jesus Christ,
meet Eldridge Cleaver." Then, turning to Cleaver,
he said, "Eldridge Cleaver, meet Jesus Christ!"
This startled Cleaver; he couldn't forget it, and in a*

few weeks he realized he had in fact come to know
Jesus Christ as his Lord and Savior.

ONE OF THE GREATEST NEEDS TODAY is for "introducers"—people who know how to put others in touch with Jesus Christ. Much of the world is aware of him, but who is going to introduce them to him? Many of us teach Sunday school, take part in Bible study groups, live ethical lives—and all of this is important. But Jesus Christ is a living person, not a formula, activity, or organization. Sharing our faith ultimately means *introducing persons to the Person*.

Andrew, one of Jesus' first band of twelve, was sort of nondescript, seldom mentioned except in a list with the other disciples. Interestingly, every time Andrew is mentioned by himself, he's introducing others to Jesus. In John 1 we read that he brought his brother to Jesus; in John 6 he brought the little boy with the loaves and fish; in John 12 he brought to Jesus some Greeks who wanted to meet him. But think what came out of those introductions: one of the greatest leaders in the New Testament—Simon Peter! One of the greatest miracles—the feeding of the five thousand! And one of the greatest statements Jesus ever made—when he saw the Greeks coming, he said, "But I, when I am lifted up from the earth, will draw all men to myself" (John 12:32).

Each of us ought to aspire to be an introducer like Andrew. Yet, as a layman said to me, "The hardest thing for most of us is actually asking someone to accept Christ." Why is that?

It is legitimate to be concerned about pushing people who are not ready. Most of us have probably known people who have been asked to receive Christ or who have walked an aisle but who gave no subsequent evidence of having accepted him or understanding the gospel. So we are sensitive, and sometimes *oversensitive*, about intruding into the lives of others.

There is a very real spiritual resistance, too. We should be aware that the devil has taken people "captive to do his will" (2 Tim. 2:26). He does not want them released and will play on our pride, fear, and oversensitivity to keep us from asking them to confess Christ.

A young manufacturer who effectively shares his faith told me he was timid about asking anyone to receive Christ for a considerable period of time. Then he realized "that if the Great Commission is true—if all authority is given to Jesus Christ—then witnessing is not my plan but his. We Christians are not asking to enter the lives of other people; Jesus Christ is. We are just his representatives."

It is tremendous to realize that we are not salesmen but co-workers with God. He is the evangelist; we are the introducers. You and I cannot convert anyone, but God can use us to help lead people to him. Jesus said, "No one can come to me unless the Father who sent me draws him" (John 6:44).

Being an introducer requires a combination of humble patience and obedient expectancy. There is no more humbling experience than being on hand when God brings someone to himself. To see God creatively break into a life freshens my own spirit! It is like observing the birth of a child. As spiritual "midwives" we need to watch how God is leading someone to himself so we may aid him.

The key word here is faith. God is going to do his work in his way in his time and will use our witness as he wants. If we really believe this, we won't manipulate people or play on their emotions. We won't try to persuade people in any way that restricts their freedom. We won't seduce people for Christ by getting them to make the right decision for the wrong reason. We will urge people lovingly, but we won't push people who are not ready. We will watch for God's moment. We will introduce everybody we can, but we will force no one.

Helping others to follow Jesus

Several years ago in Seattle a friend offered to drive me from downtown to the airport. A new freeway had opened the day before, cutting the driving time in half. It was so new they had not yet put up the access signs. For at least twenty minutes we drove all around and under the freeway until we finally found the ramp. What a frustrating experience to see those other cars whizzing by and yet not know how to get on!

Many people go through this same kind of frustration spiritually. They see Christians living a fulfilled life. They have become convinced that Jesus Christ is the Way. They want to follow him, but don't know how to begin.

How can we help them?

Mark 1: 14-17 states clearly what is involved in becoming a Christian.

"Jesus went into Galilee, proclaiming the good news of God. 'The time has come,' he said. 'The kingdom of God is near. Repent and believe the good news!'

"As Jesus walked beside the Sea of Galilee, he saw Simon and his brother Andrew casting a net into the lake, for they were fishermen. 'Come, follow me,' Jesus said, 'and I will make you fishers of men.' "

Jesus first declared what God had done in the gospel; then he spelled out what people must do. He put that demand into three imperatives:

1. Repent.
2. Believe the gospel.
3. Follow me.

Step 1 is thus a sense of need and a willingness to change.

Two New Testament words are translated "repent" in our English Bibles. The first means "to turn," an about-face, or change of direction. The second word literally means "after-thought" or to "change your mind." Repentance happens when Jesus Christ steps in front of my life, and I realize I am going the wrong way, slide over, and let him take the steering wheel and make a U-turn.

Many people think repentance involves great emotion. For some, it may; for others, it may not. What is most important is the change in mind.

The Christians in Thessalonica experienced repentance. Paul recalled that "you turned to God from idols to serve the living and true God" (1 Thess. 1: 9). Notice that they turned:

• "to God"—a positive recognition of his Lordship
• "from idols"—a negative renunciation of sin
• "to serve God"—a reorientation of life around God's will.

Repentance involves not only a new attitude toward sin but also a new attitude toward God. Repentance is a renunciation of sin because of a recognition of God. It is moving from the kingdom of self to the Kingdom of God.

What is sin? It is repudiating the living and true God and going into the God-business for ourselves. Someone who is coming to Christ must do more than recognize *sins;* he must be convicted of *sin.* Sins are what we do; sin is what we are. When I am leading people in a prayer of commitment and say, "Lord, forgive my *sin,*" they often respond, "Lord, forgive my *sins.*" But the sins we commit—the stealing, lying, cheating, and immorality—are but symptoms of the cancer of sin. They are signs that we have pushed God to the edge of our lives or ignored him altogether.

How do we help an inquirer sense his need and want to change?

Actually, the conviction of sin is God's work, not ours. We can't convict someone by abusing him, shouting at him, or trying to make him feel guilty. We can make him feel bad, but the feeling will either go away or remain to haunt him without positive change. But when the Holy Spirit brings conviction (as promised in John 16: 8-11), it is more than just being sorry about the mess we have made. As Ralph Neighbour says, "Conviction is the result of the Holy Spirit at work within the life. He brings the awareness of (1) what I am—a sinner; (2) what God is—righteous; and (3) how impossible the gulf is—judgment. Conviction . . . is a condition of God-given sorrow of personal rebellion to His Lordship."[1]

You and I cannot create this awareness; however, we can pray that God will put us in touch with those in whose lives he is working.

The first traces of conviction may be evident in relation to personal problems—fear of death, loneliness, lack of purpose, some weakness or bad habit in their lives, their concern over evil in the world.

From that problem, we help them see that their real need is for repentance from sin (singular). In other words, we have to explain that the basic problem is not the cobweb but the spider!

One of the primary ways God brings conviction is through talking about Christ. Here is an imaginary dialogue between Jim, a Christian, and Tom, a non-Christian.

TOM: Jim, I really don't understand why you're so concerned about my becoming a Christian. Why do you think I need Jesus?

JIM: Are you saying you really don't see any need of Christ?

TOM: Well, he was a good teacher and all that, but I really think my life stacks up as good as anyone else's.

JIM: Doesn't it depend on what the standard is? It's a little bit like high jumping. If I put the bar at six inches, I can jump over it every time and think, "Boy, I'm a great high jumper." But suppose I put it up there where world class high jumpers do— over seven feet. Then I stand back and look at it and say, "Hey, I'm not so good."

TOM: I get the point, but what is the standard?"

JIM: That's a good question. God has given us some negative standards, such as, "Don't kill, don't steal, don't commit adultery," and so forth, but Jesus Christ added to them. He said sin isn't only committing adultery but also lusting in your heart for a woman. The most important thing is that Jesus Christ is the only one who perfectly lived the Ten Commandments. So I have to measure my life against his.

TOM: You mean Jesus Christ is the standard?

JIM: Let's look at Romans 3: 23. It says, "All have sinned and fall short of the glory of God." What do you think is "the glory of God"?

TOM: I haven't the foggiest idea.

JIM: Well, it's God's perfection as he showed it to us one time in Jesus Christ. So really for God to accept us, it isn't enough just to be decent or as good as everyone else; we have to be as good as Jesus Christ.

TOM: Well, if *that's* the standard . . ."

A good follow-up would be for Jim to suggest that Tom read the Gospel of Mark or of John to see what kind of person Jesus Christ really was.

Another approach is to ask the person to look into his life and answer honestly, "What is the most important thing in life for me? Is it really God?"

This question could be used in connection with the first and greatest commandment. For example:

TOM: Jim, I've been pretty decent. I've kept most of the Ten Commandments most of the time.

JIM: How about the first commandment?

TOM: I'm not sure what it is.

JIM: Jesus said the first and greatest commandment is to love the Lord your God with all your heart and all your soul and all your mind and all your strength. Have you done that?

TOM: I'm not sure.

JIM: Then let me ask, what is the most important thing in your life? What do you think about again and again? Being great . . . successful . . . your problems or jealousies? When you're alone, is there something that keeps coming back to the center of your mind like a ball on a rubber string? Whatever you think about most is probably the god you really worship instead of the true God.

Jim Kennedy, now pastor of the Coral Ridge Presbyterian Church in Florida and creator of the worldwide Evangelism Explosion program, was once an Arthur Murray dance instructor. He turned on the radio one Sunday morning and heard the late Dr. Donald Barnhouse give a message based on the question, "If you should stand before God, and he said, 'Why should I allow you into my heaven?' what would you say?" Kennedy's interest was aroused. He heard Barnhouse list the reasons the average person would give—I have gone to church, I have done good works, I have believed in God, I have tried to treat my neighbor right, I have never done anything terribly bad. . . . Then Barnhouse pointed out that it is impossible for a perfect God to let sin into his presence. As Kennedy realized the impossible demands of God, he saw his need for a Savior. He has since used this question many times, and it has become a standard question that many Christians use in presenting the gospel.

The late Paul Little used an analogy that could go like this:

TOM: Well, I'm not perfect, but I think I'm as good as a lot of other people, and better than some.

JIM: That may be true, but put it like this. Suppose we all lined up on the West Coast to swim to Hawaii. One person might only get 25 yards from the beach. Someone else might make 100 yards. If you're a good swimmer, you might make five miles. But who's going to make it to Hawaii?

TOM: Nobody.

JIM: In the same way, I may be better than somebody else, but I still come short as far as God is concerned.

When we are talking about sin, our attitude is extremely important. Without gentleness and honest humility about ourselves, we will just make people mad by seeming to put them down. We are not angels condescending to lesser creatures. A man told me he kept away from Christ for a long time because his wife seemed so perfect he knew he couldn't be like that. If she had shared her own weaknesses, he might have responded sooner.

Remember that conviction of sin is the work of the Holy Spirit. We need to use the Word of God so that people measure themselves against his standard. And the most important thing is to pray until that sense of need comes.

Not everybody has a deep conviction of sin *before* he comes to Christ. Sometimes the sense of need may come before there is a sense of sin. People from Christian backgrounds often have a sense of guilt before conversion; others may not. They turn to Jesus Christ to be freed from habits and fears or to fix a broken marriage, and they find Jesus as Liberator before they recognize him as Savior from sin. In either case, we ought to be careful to identify specific areas of need in their lives of which they are aware and which they are willing to let God change.

Step 2: Believe the gospel.

The gospel is basically the good news that God has done in Jesus Christ what we could never do for ourselves. To believe is to put our full confidence and trust in the truthfulness of the gospel.

How do we convey this? The late Paul Little emphasized:

Because the gospel is about a person, there is no rigid and rote way in which it is to be presented. Whenever we are talking about a person rather than a formula, we always begin with that aspect of the person's appearance, character and personality that are the most relevant at the moment. If you have a blond brother who is studying chemistry at Harvard and you meet someone who is also studying at Harvard, you don't begin the conversation by saying, "I have a brother who is blond, is studying chemistry, and is at Harvard." Rather, you begin, "Oh, I have a brother who is at Harvard," and you may then go to the other facts as they are relevant. On the other hand, if you meet someone who is almost an identical twin to your brother, you wouldn't begin by saying that you have a brother who is studying chemistry. Rather you might say, "You look just like my brother," and then go on to other facts.

In the same way, when we are talking about the Lord Jesus Christ, it may be that at one time His resurrection is the most relevant aspect of His person and work. Another time it might be His death, another His diagnosis of human nature, and another time who He is. Eventually, we want to cover all the information in the gospel. We must be conversant with the basic facts about the Lord Jesus Christ that a person ought to know to become a Christian, and it is imperative to know where these can be documented in the New Testament.[2]

Jesus used the words "I am" a number of times in the Gospel of John. Consider how some of these relate to basic human needs:

- Emptiness—"I am the bread of Life" (John 6: 35).
- Purposelessness—"I am the light of the world. Whoever follows me will never walk in darkness" (John 8: 12).
- Fear of death—"I am the resurrection and the life" (John 11: 25).
- Truth—"I am the way—the truth, and the life" (John 14: 6).

We have to recognize, of course, that many other gurus, prophets, and self-appointed saviors today are saying, "I am." Some even teach that each of us can claim to be the "I am," that all of us are "sons of God." So when we present the claims of Jesus Christ, we need to stress three unique points:

1. He claimed uniquely to be *the* Son of God, not just *a* son of God (John 5: 18; John 10: 10-30; John 14: 9). John 3: 16 says that Jesus Christ was the "only begotten son." A carpenter may create a table, but he begets a son. You and I have been created by God, and when we receive Jesus Christ we are born again as sons of God. But Jesus Christ is God's "only begotten" son. That is, he is the only one who is God by his very nature.

2. Jesus Christ came uniquely to die "for forgiveness of sins" (Matt. 26: 28; see also 1 Cor. 15: 3-4). What is distinctive to the Christian faith is that God actually became man to die for us and take the death penalty for our sins, substituting for our guilt in order that he might bring us back to God (see 1 Pet. 3: 18).

3. He uniquely rose from the dead. Luke 24: 36-48 shows Jesus appearing to the disciples. They were scared to death and thought he must be a ghost. But Jesus said, "Touch me and see;

a ghost does not have flesh and bones, as you see I have" (vs. 39). No skeptic has been able to explain how the first Christians, who were defeated and discouraged when Jesus died, were transformed into mighty witnesses. The change can't be explained—unless Jesus really did rise from the dead!

Step 3: Follow me.

Faith is more than intellectual assent to what Jesus was. Genuine faith is a personal relationship to what Jesus is. As someone has put it, "In becoming a Christian, there is *something* to believe, *someone* to receive."

Compare faith to marriage. Marriage is more than a philosophy or institution. It is a relationship. I may study the historical development and sociological implications of marriage. But unless I have a partner with whom I am personally related, I am not married. So someone may study Christianity and still not have a personal relationship with Jesus.

Faith in Jesus Christ is a personal commitment based on the truth we have come to know about him. Our imaginary conversation might proceed like this:

JIM: Tom, does what I have shared with you make any sense?

TOM: Yes, it really does.

JIM: Would you mind sharing with me why?

TOM: You really put your finger today, Jim, on what is wrong in my life. Things have really been going rough, and I've been trying to blame everybody else. You know Peg and I have been having problems. Well, I thought it was just that we needed a bigger home, and things would get better when the children came along. But when Krissy came, things still weren't right. I thought if I worked hard and made more money things would improve, but I found I'd just become a workaholic. I'm just getting tighter and tighter, and I've really been having some conflicts at work. The more we've talked, the more I've seen that I've put me—Tom—at the center of my life.

JIM: Would you like to open your life to Jesus Christ, Tom?

TOM: I would, but how? I've never understood how that happens. I've never had one of those born-again experiences, if that's what you mean. Do I just wait for some kind of emotional flash to hit me?

JIM: Let me share two verses that might help. *(He asks Tom to read John 1:12, 13 silently and then out loud.)* There are three important verbs in these verses—*believe, receive,* and *become.*

TOM: Right.

JIM: Those are active verbs. It's just like getting married. Tom, when you and Peggy fell in love, you *believed* she was the girl for you. So you *received* her, and you *became* husband and wife. Is that correct?

TOM: Correct.

JIM: Well, it's like that with Jesus Christ. You *believe* what he claimed to be—the Son of God who died for your sin. You *receive* him into your life by a personal invitation. And as a result, you *become* a son of God.

TOM: So I have to really try to believe in Jesus Christ?

JIM: I wouldn't say "try." The word I would use is "trust." Faith in Jesus Christ is not something you achieve. It is more something you receive. It is like receiving a gift, but in this case the gift is a person.

TOM: So if I have enough faith, Jesus Christ will come into my life?

JIM: Let me put it like this. It isn't faith that saves us. It is Jesus Christ. Faith is like the coupling that joins a locomotive to the cars. The coupling doesn't do the pulling, the engine does. The coupling just joins it.

And if they want to receive Christ—then what?

A young lady wrote to me, "If I talk to someone about Christ and they want to accept Christ, then what do I do? That is what really scares me about talking to someone. I don't know what to do."

You may feel the same. Of course, you can always introduce your friend to someone else you feel can lead them. But one of the greatest privileges you can have is to be on hand when someone comes to know Jesus Christ. I would encourage you to have the faith to step out and let God continue to use you.

How? Should we try to get the person to pray in our presence? There isn't any standard answer. "Praying to receive Christ" is not an essential part of salvation, though it may be an important expression of that salvation. As Romans 10:9 indicates, *we believe in our hearts and confess with our mouths.* Faith may be born in the depths of a person even as we talk about Jesus Christ. Others may need a focus for their faith, and we can help to lead them in prayer. We have to be sensitive to the occasion, the person, and the leading of the Holy Spirit.

Pro golfer Rik Massengale and his wife Cindy talked with me for about fifteen minutes after Billy Graham spoke to the golf tour Bible study. They had a number of questions. A year later they told me they had gone back to their room and had prayed together, asking God to take over their lives. I didn't ask them to do that, but God led them to it.

On a pack trip in Colorado, one man was impressed by the relationship to Jesus Christ he had seen in a friend. We talked about what it meant to know Christ personally as we rode along the trail that day. Around the campfire that night, we sang and shared. As it came time to turn in, someone said, "Let's have a prayer." He turned to this guy and said, "Bill, why don't you lead us?"

Bill stood, looked around the campfire, and said, "Men, I would just like to say what a wonderful day this has been. It has been so great being out here in this beautiful creation and being with fellows like you. It's wonderful to sing and talk openly about our families and the purpose of our lives. I just want to thank God for this. And I want Jesus Christ to be in my life as I have seen him in yours." He said all of this looking straight at us, his eyes wide open.

When he finished, one of the group said, "That's great, Bill. Now, lead us in prayer."

"That *was* my prayer," Bill answered. He didn't know you were supposed to bow your head, close your eyes, and say words that sounded a certain way. It was beautiful to see this natural expression of his coming to faith.

When you feel someone is ready for commitment, you might say something like this:

JIM: Would you like to open your life to Christ and begin a relationship with him?

TOM: Jim, I really would.

JIM: Well, why don't you tell God that he hasn't been in the center of your life, and what it is you have specifically put first. If your hands are full of stones and I want to give you a gift, you have to be willing to drop the stones in order to get the gift.

TOM: Okay. I'm ready to tell God I will let those "stones"

drop—try not to play God with my family and everybody else.

JIM: Well, then, Tom, Jesus Christ is with you right now through his Holy Spirit. Ask him to come into your life, to forgive you, and to show you how to live for him.

Now, what do you do at this point? Consider these options:

1. You can suggest that the person get alone some place; tell him the kind of prayer to pray, and then ask him to tell you about it afterward.

2. Encourage him to pray aloud in the presence of a witness, and, in many cases, to go ahead and kneel in a sense of reverence and humility before God. Just as marriage vows are exchanged publicly, a shared expression clinches a decision. The "yes" someone says to Jesus is like a nail driven through a board. The shared expression is like clinching that nail on the other side so it does not pull back easily. However, whether or not someone prays with you depends entirely on the mood, the person, and the circumstances.

Then you might lead the person in a prayer like the one that follows—pausing and letting him repeat the words themselves. Encourage him to pray the words out loud, but if he prefers to do it silently, that's okay.

Dear God, I am coming to you right now the best I know how. . . . I believe that you made this world and that you made me. . . . I believe that you have a destiny for my life. . . . I know that I have sinned and put myself first. . . . I am sorry and I want to turn from sin to you. . . . I believe that Jesus Christ, your Son, came into this world . . . that he died for my sin and rose again. . . . Jesus Christ, take my life right now. . . . Please come in and live in me. . . . Forgive my sin. . . . Live your life through me. . . . Help me to follow you.

Following this, whether he has prayed silently or out loud, encourage the person to pray in his own words:

JIM: Tom, you have asked Jesus Christ to come into your life. I wonder if there is anything you specifically want to confess that has been wrong. Why don't you tell him?

(Tom prays silently or out loud if there is anything he specifically wants forgiveness for.

JIM: Someone has said that faith is when you stop saying please and start saying thank you. If you have really come to

Jesus Christ and trusted him, he has come into your life. He said, "Whoever comes to me I will never drive away" (John 6: 37). If you have come to him, he has received you. Why don't you just thank him?

(Tom expresses thanks in his own words.)

JIM: Is there something you really want God to help you with? Why not ask him for strength?

(Tom asks God for help in some special area of need.)

At this point, each individual's response will differ. Some people have a great sense of joy. Other people weep, particularly if they have been under emotional pressure and have been struggling for a long time. Others just have a quiet peace and assurance. Some don't feel anything in particular.

After a few moments of quietness, I usually say, "Has Jesus Christ come into your life? Has God made himself real to you?"

Usually if the Holy Spirit has really been at work, the person will answer, "Yes, I think so" or "Yes, he has."

I then reply, "How do you know?"

The answer will often be "Because I feel better (or cleaner, or freer)" or "I just feel good."

Don't discourage that feeling! Ask the person to be thankful to God. But point out that while feelings are good, they are not the basis of our assurance. We have a relationship with Christ based on who he is and what he has done, not just on our emotions.

JIM: Tom, that's great. I'm glad you have that feeling. But suppose you wake up tomorrow and you're sick, or you break your leg skiing. Will Christ still be there?

TOM: Yes, I believe he will.

JIM: How do you know?

TOM: Well, I'm not really sure.

JIM: Tom, I think it is important that you understand what your faith is based on. It can't be based on what I say, because I won't always be around. It can't be based on your feelings, because your feelings are always changing. What you really need to base your faith on is the character of God as we find it in the Bible. Let me give you an illustration. *(Jim pulls out a pen.)* Suppose I said, "I'm going to give you this pen tomorrow," and you went home and told Peggy, and she replied, "How do you know?" What would you say?

Tom: I would say, "Jim told me."

Jim: So it would depend on two things—did I tell you, and could you trust me?

Tom: That's right.

Jim: Well, it's the same with Jesus Christ. Let's look again at John 6: 37, where Jesus said, "Whoever comes to me I will never drive away." Tom, who said that?

Tom: Jesus.

Jim: Have you come to Jesus Christ?

Tom: Yes, I have.

Jim: Then will he drive you away?

Tom: No.

Jim: Well, has he received you then?

Tom: I think so.

Jim: How do you know?

Tom: Well, I just feel he has.

Jim: Again, Tom, that's great, but I want to stress who is it that said if you came to him, he wouldn't drive you away.

Tom: It was Jesus.

Jim: Can you believe him?

Tom: I can.

Jim: Is his word going to change?

Tom: No, it isn't.

Jim: Well, then, how do you know he has received you?

Tom: I know because Jesus Christ said it, and I can trust him.

All this is far more than an exercise of words. When Christ comes into a life, changes take place. They may not necessarily be dramatic, but they are definite and very specific. New believers begin to love Jesus. They want to obey his commandments, read his Word, communicate with him, share their faith, and love other believers as Christ has loved them. In other words, genuine faith in Jesus Christ leads to his fruits being reproduced in the life of the new Christian.

It is my prayer that everyone who reads this book will at some point have the privilege of saying to another person, "I would like you to meet Jesus Christ," and of seeing that transforming friendship begin.

    1. Ralph Neighbour, *The Touch of the Spirit* (Nashville: Broadman, 1972), pp. 145-46.
    2. Little, *How to Give Away Your Faith* (Downers Grove, Ill.: InterVarsity, 1966), pp. 56-57.

How Do I Get Started?

"DO I REALLY HAVE TO MASTER everything in this book before I start to share my faith?" you may wonder.

Of course not. It would be good to review and absorb as much as you can. But just as you learn tennis best by playing, so you learn evangelism best by actually sharing.

Now is the time to venture. Here are a few specific thoughts on how you can get started.

1. Build on the concern God has given to you. It's easy to read a book about evangelism but far more scary actually to share your faith with someone else. The fact that you still feel reluctant may make you feel guilty. You may try to psyche yourself up: "If I love God, and if people are lost, and if I believe the gospel is true, I ought to be a real gung-ho, on-fire witness." But are you still a little bit overwhelmed?

The fact that you even bothered to read this book shows God has already given to you a positive attitude and a desire to share your faith. So don't put yourself down. Thank God instead for what you have learned through reading and in many other ways. Think about some of the positive instances in which you have been able to witness for Christ or influence someone toward him. He is already working in your life!

2. Put yourself in a situation that will be conducive to sharing your faith. Find a group of Christians who are excited about doing just that.

In my evangelistic crusades, we frequently invite a team of lay people to share their faith at breakfast meetings, coffee hours, and late-night gatherings in homes. A businessman from

Canada once confessed why he'd always found an excuse to get out of our invitation to join one of these teams. He was scared. "I have always witnessed by proxy or by check," he admitted ruefully. "I have served on many boards and have given to many Christian enterprises, but I have never been personally involved in witnessing."

Finally, he and his wife became part of a team of lay people who really had something to share, and God worked in their lives. I remember the night they came back from a session with a group of young people. They were so excited they could hardly sleep. This probably would never have happened if they had not allowed themselves to join a group committed to evangelism.

Look for such a group within your own church and ask to be part of it. If your church doesn't have one, try to find some other Christian fellowship that is committed to evangelism, and become a part of it.

Begin where it is relatively easy to talk about Jesus Christ. God does not necessarily want you to start by witnessing to Fidel Castro! Jesus once talked about soil that had been prepared for the good seed of the gospel. Try to involve yourself in a situation where you are likely to find receptive people. In the crusades conducted by the Billy Graham Team and other evangelists, many people get their first experience of sharing their faith by serving as counselors. They find it relatively easy to talk with people who have come forward publicly in a crusade setting, thus indicating their openness and receptivity. If such an opportunity comes your way, take it!

A social worker from Pennsylvania came as part of a tourist group to attend a crusade we held on a small Caribbean island. On the beach one day, he said to me, "I have always found it difficult to talk about my faith. But down here it has been so easy. The crusade has made these people very interested. Any place I have gone on the island, I have been able to talk to people, and I've found them so open. This is my first experience at being able to verbalize what Christ means to me."

3. *Ask someone to show you how to get started.* If you want to know how to fly, you go to a flight instructor. If you want to know how to play chess, you ask an experienced player or a pro to show you. Look among your Christian friends or the leaders

of your church or fellowship. Find someone who seems to have God-given gifts in this area. Ask to go with them sometime when they will be speaking with someone about Christ. Watch them. As baseball player and manager Yogi Berra said, "You observe a lot by watching!"

Jim Kennedy began the famed Evangelism Explosion program at Coral Ridge Presbyterian Church in just this way. At first he gave lectures on evangelism. Nothing happened. Then he remembered that the way he had learned was from a fellow pastor who took Jim along in house-to-house visiting. So Jim began to take one lay person for several weeks, then another and another. As they watched him, they gained confidence and knowledge.

Ask your teacher to give you a chance to witness while he watches you, and to give you suggestions. It takes humility sometimes to do this—but it takes humility to be a good witness. I met a pastor who had had no evangelistic training in seminary. He was absolutely frustrated by his inability to communicate the gospel when making calls. So he went to one of his laymen who was an outstanding personal evangelist and said, "I don't know how to do what you do. Will you teach me?" The layman said he would be glad to. One afternoon a week for several months he met with the pastor, prayed with him, instructed him, took him along, and let the pastor watch how he introduced people to Christ. Now that pastor, having learned, has a new dimension of effectiveness in his own evangelistic ministry.

If you don't know or can't find somebody to do this in your church, pray that God will lead you to someone or to a program where you can learn. Many denominations and Christian organizations now have excellent seminars in witnessing.

4. Get specific. Taking Christ to the world has to begin with taking Christ to the person next door or to someone in your neighborhood. Look over the following list of very specific things you can start doing. Add other actions that are possibilities for you:

- Make a list of one to five people you know who evidence a need for Christ.
- Start to pray for them daily.
- Plan some specific friendship activity with one or more of these persons.

- Mention some of your Christian activities as you're talking with them.
- Send Christ-honoring Christmas or Easter cards.
- Invite them to church.
- Invite them to a Christian event.
- Give them a Christian book or article.
- Write out your testimony, and share it first with a Christian friend and then a non-Christian.
- Do the same with the presentation of the gospel.

5. *Most important, act—and do it now!* Studies of human behavior have shown that when we are faced with a responsibility we know we ought to accept, and we do nothing about it, it becomes harder for us to act than before. Having read this book, if you do nothing about it, you may be worse off than when you started. I say gently but seriously that, having learned what you have learned, you now have a greater responsibility before God to share it in some way.

However, it need not be a big way. The journey's first step may be a small one. Remember that God has said, "Go into all your worlds," and "As you go, make disciples."

Who is the person—or persons—for whom God has given you a specific concern? Pray about them right now. Visualize those persons in your mind right now. Write down their names in the following space right now.

What is the first step you believe God wants you to take to share your faith with this (these) person(s)? Read through the list above. Ask God to direct you to any of those or any other steps. Stop right now and meditate on it. What is it that God wants you to do? Write it down in the following space and be very specific.

When will you do what God has told you to do? Stop and think. Be realistic about the time involved. But don't procrastinate. When will you begin to take this first step? Write it down in this space: _____

Now pray about this step constantly. Make yourself some kind of a reminder. Write it down as a covenant, and put it some place where you will see it. Share this specific step you are going to take with some Christian, and ask him to pray with you about the results.

You will need to evaluate what has happened, to reflect on it, and to decide the next step. In the following space, write down what did or didn't happen, and the next step God would have you take.

Good news *is* for sharing!
Now that you've started, keep going, and remember God will be with you every step until the end of the age. So don't keep the faith to yourself—pass it on!

APPENDIX

Questions, Questions

THE LATE PAUL LITTLE was one of the most experienced student evangelists of our generation. After conducting literally hundreds of question-and-answer sessions with various groups, he found that only rarely did he encounter a question he had not run into many times before. He categorized them into seven groups:

1. "What about the heathen who have never heard of Christ—are they going to hell?"
2. "Is Christ the only way to God?"
3. "Why do the innocent suffer?"
4. "How can miracles be possible?"
5. "Isn't the Bible full of errors?"
6. "Isn't Christian experience only psychological?"
7. "Won't a good moral life get me to heaven?"

Little's suggested answers to these questions may be found in chapter 5, "Why We Believe," of his book *How To Give Away Your Faith,* published by InterVarsity Press. They are spelled out at greater length in his later book, *Know Why You Believe,* also from InterVarsity.

This appendix presents a similar list of questions I have faced and suggests ways for Christians to respond.

"Why do I need Jesus Christ?"

All of us have friends, neighbors, and acquaintances who show no sense of interest. Materialists, skeptics, atheists, agnostics, religious people, decent moral people—all of them may say, "Thanks, but no thanks."

C. S. Lewis, the brilliant English Christian, was for many years an atheist. Yet, in his autobiography, *Surprised by Joy,* he revealed that as a young atheist he found it hard to keep up his defenses, because God was constantly pressing in on his life from every angle, until finally

Lewis could no longer ignore him! God has not left himself without a witness to any person.

Our primary responsibility is to be sensitive to those many people around us in whose lives God is already at work and who sense their need. Yet at the same time we also ought to ask him to show himself so real in our lives that this will make others want to know the dimension of living we have discovered.

Further, when we as Christians sensitively listen to other people, we often find an unspoken and sometimes unrealized need. Eldridge Cleaver told me that even as a thoroughgoing Marxist he was troubled by the fact that he could not find in that materialistic philosophy any basis for the justice he so passionately wanted in the world. Dr. Boris Dotsenko was head of the nuclear physics department at the University of Kiev in the Ukraine. Though officially a Marxist, through his scientific studies he came to believe there must be a spiritual power to keep the material universe from running down. Torn by this seeming contradiction with his atheism, he was on the verge of committing suicide when he realized that if God existed, he could reveal himself to him. Dotsenko began a search that ultimately ended when, reading a Gideon Bible in a hotel room in Canada, he came to realize who God was and how to find him.

The sense of need is primarily related to understanding that God is, who he is, and what he is like. We need to listen carefully to understand where people are in their belief or unbelief about God. Then we must probe gently but insistently, asking questions to uncover their presuppositions and beliefs, and leading them in turn to ask the kinds of questions God may use to bring them to himself.

When someone says, "That faith stuff is okay for you, but I don't need it; I'm an atheist," there are several possible lines of reply. I might say, "Tell me about the God you don't believe in. Maybe I don't believe in him either." A lot of people have a major misconception of who God is. We need to find out what it is about God that they are rejecting.

At the University of Virginia, folksinger John Fischer, black evangelist Tom Skinner, and I were invited to take part in a series called "Jesus Christ vs. Christianity." In preparation, the Christians asked a number of students to complete the statement "When I think of Christianity, I think of . . ." I began my first talk by reading what one student had written: "When I think of Christianity, I think of the Crusades, the Thirty Years' War, the Ku Klux Klan, racial segregation, etc., etc."

The last night of the meetings a gentle, long-haired guy came up and said, "You remember that statement you read the first night?"

"Yes," I said.

"Well, I wrote it."

"You did?"

"Yes," he said, "and tonight I became a Christian." He had rejected not real Christianity but a God he saw as a symbol of bigotry and prejudice. Then, embodied in a team of Christian speakers from different cultural and racial backgrounds, he sensed genuine love and responded to the God who really is.

Ask a professed atheist, "How much do you know of everything there is to know? Einstein said that he knew less than half of one percent. How about you?" Asked with a smile and without sarcasm, this question will usually bring an honest answer. You may then continue, "Well, is it possible that God exists in the amount of reality that you yourself haven't yet personally explored or encountered?" This can be the opening as to whether this person would like to know God if he does exist.

"How can a good God tolerate a world of evil and suffering?"

As the couplet goes, "If God is God, he is not good; if God is good, he is not God."

I have not yet read an explanation of the problem of evil that satisfied me, and I don't expect to until I get to heaven. I find it helpful to admit to the questioner that I do not have an answer fully satisfactory to myself, and yet to point out that if we use the existence of evil to say there is no God, we wind up with other problems. Once I talked with a young Jewish man who said it was inconceivable to him that God could exist and let Hitler kill 7 million Jews. After we parted, it suddenly occurred to me that I wish I had asked him, "If there is no God, what was wrong with Hitler killing 7 million Jews?"

Once we have said we don't believe in God, we have another problem: Why then is there a difference between good and evil? Dostoevski, the Russian novelist, said, "If there is no God, then anything is permitted."

"Why did God make us if he knew we would sin?"

A student asked me that at a university lecture. "God must have thought you and I were worth the risk," I replied. I pointed out that love between my wife and me would be meaningless if she were like a doll and all I had to do was push a button to get her to say, "I love you—please kiss me." To be meaningful, love has to be given freely. God has created us to love and obey him because we want to, not because we have to. Otherwise, morality is meaningless.

But once God opened this door, he also opened the option of man sinning, rebelling, and causing evil, suffering, hatred, and war in the world.

"Then why doesn't God stamp out evil?"

He could if he wanted to. But as Paul Little perceptively asked, "If God decided to stamp out all evil at midnight tonight, how many of us would be here at one in the morning?" Evil is not just "out there" in the world. It is "in here"—in me. Man, not God, is responsible for the selfishness and injustice that causes so much of the evil we see.

C. S. Lewis has dealt perceptively with right and wrong as a clue to the meaning of the universe in part 1 of his book *The Case for Christianity*. This is well worth reading and rereading, for the atheist has the task of explaining where the sense of right and wrong comes from if there is no God who is the base for morality.

In similar fashion we can ask the atheist to explain how love and freedom and joy and significance came about in a world without God. Francis Schaeffer uses the analogy of the universe being like a great room filled with water. We humans are fish swimming in this self-contained ocean. Then imagine that suddenly we evolve lungs, which need oxygen. Here we are, suddenly gasping for breath, a part of us having a need that cannot be met. In effect, that is the situation in which the atheist finds himself. He has a need for love, freedom, and significance, and yet no reason in a completely materialistic world to believe that such things exist. Yet he cannot live this way. He longs for love. He experiences joy. He may be concerned about injustice. He looks for the significance of his life.

We have to prayerfully keep pushing the unbeliever until he sees he cannot live consistently with what he says he believes.

Some atheists, Julian Huxley for one, go so far as to say that though there is no God, human beings function better if they act as though God exists. To which Francis Schaeffer comments, "These thinkers are saying in effect that man can only function as man for an extended period of time if he acts on the assumption that a lie (that the personal God of Christianity is there) is true. You cannot find any deeper despair than this for a sensitive person."[1]

"I'm not sure whether God exists or not."

Most thoughtful skeptics agree that they are really agnostics rather than atheists. J. Edwin Orr suggests that we ask the agnostic, "Are you an ordinary agnostic or an ornery agnostic?" What's the difference? "Well," explains Orr, "an ordinary agnostic says, 'I don't know whether God exists or not,' but an ornery one says, 'I don't know, and nobody can know.' "

To which Orr replies, "How can you be so sure that I don't know!"

It's important to stress to an agnostic that, in biblical Christianity, God takes the initiative. Communication doesn't flow first from man to God, but vice versa. God took the first step to create the world, and, according to John 1: 14, God has taken the first step to communicate his reality through Jesus Christ in the space-time world of human beings. I sometimes put it like this:

"You and I sit here talking in these two chairs. Now we can know those chairs by observation. We can take a piece of wood out of the chair, test it in a laboratory, analyze it, and know pretty much what the chair is. But I can't know you by observation. I can tell some things about you—you're red-haired, have freckles, are about 5' 11'', and weigh 155 pounds. But I couldn't really know you if you hadn't taken the trouble to come to me, introduce yourself, and ask me your questions. That is always true in communication between people. We have to decide to reveal ourselves if we are going to have any kind of communication. The same thing is true with God. We can tell some things about God as Creator from looking inside ourselves, seeing our conscience, looking at the universe around us, and knowing there has to be some great power, design, and purpose. But the only way we can ever know God is if he decides to take the initiative and to communicate with us."

"But how do I know whether God has spoken? I've never heard him speak."

This is the place to introduce the concept of God showing himself in history in the person of Jesus. After all, he claimed that "anyone who has seen me has seen the Father" (John 14: 9). We also need to make it clear that in the Bible we believe we have an accurate record of this disclosure God has made. At this point we need not ask anyone to affirm that the Bible is the inspired Word of God. We only need to ask that it be taken as an accurate historical record of what Jesus Christ was and what he said.

It is often good to ask, "If God exists, would you like to get to know him?" A young lady taking part in a discussion group led by Stuart Briscoe brashly asserted she was an atheist.

"Do you know everything?" he asked.

"No."

"Then is it possible that God exists outside of what you know?"

"Yes, it is."

"Well, then," he said, "you aren't an atheist; you're an agnostic. Would you like to know God if he does exist?"

She replied that she would.

"Well," he smiled, "you've come to the right place. You're not an agnostic—you're a seeker!"

Many genuine agnostics want to know how to seek sincerely but honestly. They may want to move from skepticism to faith, but they can't take a dishonest step and say they believe in what they don't believe. At this point it helps to suggest what might be called an experiment of faith, just as a laboratory scientist tries to verify a colleague's hypothesis. He doesn't say at the beginning that he accepts it, but he goes through certain experiments that will help him conclude whether or not this hypothesis has any validity.

Jesus said, "If a man chooses to do God's will, he will find out whether my teaching comes from God or whether I speak on my own" (John 7:17). If an agnostic is willing to do God's will, then God promises to reveal whether Jesus Christ is just another man or whether he really speaks the truth of God.

My challenge would go like this: "If you really want to know whether God is, make this experiment. Pray as honestly as you can, 'God, I'm not sure if you are really there. But if you are, I know you can hear me, and I really do want to know you. If you will reveal yourself to me and what your will is for my life, I am willing to follow it. If you will show me that Jesus Christ is the truth, I'm willing to follow him wherever it may lead.' " Then I suggest to the person that the New Testament documents claim to tell us the truth about Christ's life, claims, offers, and demands. Will he read through one of the Gospels, a chapter or more a day, and ask constantly, "Who is Jesus? What does he teach? What is he saying to me?" I also suggest that the person put into action the things Jesus Christ is saying, insofar as he senses Christ speaking. "Commit as much of yourself as you know to as much of Jesus Christ as you know" can be a helpful beginning.

If someone can believe in Jesus Christ at this point only as a good man or a prophet, let him start there—and I believe God will take him on to understand full reality. After all, the Samaritan woman started by calling Jesus "sir," went on to recognize that he was "a prophet," and ended up asking if he were not "the Christ" (John 4:11, 19, 29).

In Kingston, Ontario, a student at the Royal Military College was bored by my address and said afterwards he spent most of the evening mentally rearranging the public address system, which was not working properly. But at the end of my talk I gave a challenge as outlined above. He was impressed. Back in his room he dug out of a bottom drawer a Bible that had been given to him when he went off to college. He began to read it, seeking honestly to know God. Several days later he wrote me to say he had discovered that Jesus Christ was real. "I was surprised," he said, "to find such a joy-filled moment in my life."

"I think God will accept anyone who's sincere."

Many people have the idea that God is a good guy, and if there is any such thing as a final judgment, he will grade on the curve. All he requires, these people feel, is that we do our best. If our good deeds outweigh our bad, we will probably make it to heaven.

These persons need to see the nature of God. God is not our big buddy upstairs. He is the God of perfect, infinite, blazing holiness.

Ad infinitum most people have heard the familiar Scripture "God is love." But how many know that the same writer in the Bible also said, "God is light; in him there is no darkness at all" (1 John 1: 5)? Light and darkness cannot live together. Where light comes, darkness goes. A perfect, holy God and sinful human beings cannot be together. That's why it is impossible for sin to come into heaven.

"How good do you have to be to get into heaven?"

As good as Jesus Christ! A student once said to a Christian, "I don't see why you Christians emphasize all that Savior stuff. I'll accept Jesus Christ as a good teacher and follow his example."

Said his Christian friend in response, "Let's take the first step. The Bible says in 1 Peter 2: 22 that Jesus Christ committed no sin, and no deceit was found in his mouth."

The student got the point. "I can't follow him," he replied. "I'm not good enough."

"I may not be perfect, but I'm better than a lot of Christians. Look at the hypocrites in the church."

The church *is* made up of imperfect people. After all, it's not a museum for stuffed saints but a hospital for those who are spiritually sick and have admitted it and come to Jesus Christ for forgiveness and changing.

We can sometimes ask, "You may have met some bad examples of Christians, but have you ever met one *real* Christian?" If the answer is yes, then we can ask, "What is it that keeps you from being the second?"

"But I've always been a Christian. I've gone to church since I was a kid."

Many nominal churchgoers have a little inoculation of Christianity, just enough to keep from getting the real thing.

An international student said, "We hear Christianity argued, debated, and criticized but never explained." Some people think a Christian is anybody who is not a Jew or an adherent of some other world religion. They're Christians, they think, because they've been born in a Christian culture. Other people think of Christianity as hereditary; if you are born in a Christian family, you are a Christian. Still others define a Christian as someone who attends a church or tries to practice the Golden Rule. To still others, a Christian is a person who gives mental assent to certain beliefs, "I believe there is a God. I believe Jesus Christ lived and died," etc.

The problem is compounded by a lack of clear teaching in some circles. How does one become a Christian? At this point a division is evident between evangelical and nonevangelical churches. The nonevangelical emphasis is basically that a person becomes a Christian by being baptized, by becoming a member of the church, by gradual Christian education. It is a process of religious osmosis. Many such people acquire a veneer of Christianity but do not discover a genuine personal relationship with Jesus Christ.

Evangelical Christians do not deny the importance and validity of the Christian family, nurture in the church, baptism, and Communion (the Lord's Supper). All of these are important. But these nurturing processes are like laying logs in a fireplace—a match has to be touched before the fire will blaze. A personal relationship to Christ requires a personal response to what God has done for us. "The gift of God is eternal life" (Rom. 6: 23), and gifts have to be received.

You can't be born a Christian any more than you can be born married. Nor is attending church enough, though it is important. As the old saying goes, "I can spend a lot of time in a garage, but that doesn't make me an automobile." Mental assent to Christian truths is vital but does not in itself make us Christians. As James says, the demons themselves believe in one God! (James 2: 19).

John 1: 12, 13 states that "to all who received him, to those who believed in his name, he gave the right to become the children of God—children born not of natural descent, nor of human decision or a husband's will, but born of God." Being a Christian is not a matter of environment, self-effort, or family background, but of God's direct action and our personal response. It was not a derelict but an upright, respectable religious leader named Nicodemus to whom Jesus said, "You must be born again." Sometimes the hardest thing for people to see is that we need to repent not of just the socially unacceptable "bad sins" but of the pride, status-seeking, class consciousness, and self-righteousness that are acceptable to society but are an abomination in God's sight.

An effective illustration is the legendary story about a man who went to heaven. At the gate he was told, "You have to have a thousand points to come in." The man was sure he would make it because he had been involved in many church and service activities. So he confidently began to recite his good works. "I went to church every Sunday, I was an officer there, and I was a member of Kiwanis and many other community activities."

"Good," came the reply, "that's two points."

"Two points!" The man's heart lurched. "Well, I also had a perfect Sunday school attendance record when I was a kid, and I was chairman of the United Fund canvass in our section one year, and I worked with the Boy Scouts."

"Fine," came the reply, "that's two more. What else?"

By now the fellow was desperate. He scraped up all he could think of, including cutting a widow's lawn when he was a kid and taking a minister out to dinner—for a grand total of six points!

Dejectedly, he finally said, "That's all I can think of. There isn't anything else. I guess I'll just have to throw myself on the grace of God."

"That's a thousand plus," came the answer. "Come on in!"

"I'm a Zen Buddhist (Scientologist, Jehovah's Witness, et al)."

How do we relate to people from various cults and new religious groups who, far from exposing their needs, are trying to convert *us?*

Certainly we need to study their beliefs. But perhaps the most basic thing is to see these not as cultists but as *people* for whom Christ died. God loves them, and they have needs, even if they don't show them. We need to listen sensitively and courteously to what they have to say about their lives and their beliefs. We can say, "I don't know too much about your beliefs. Why don't you tell me? I'm interested." Then, having listened, we can ask for an equal opportunity to share with them. There will still be a hunger inside them to know God with certainty, even though they may have found a system that partially satisfies. A straightforward testimony of the assurance of eternal life that Jesus Christ gives, offered without argument, may be the means of reaching such a person.

"Can Jesus Christ meet my needs?"

Many people have never really gotten a clear picture of Jesus. They have picked up all kinds of caricatures:

- the revolutionary Jesus, a Bible in one hand and a Molotov cocktail in the other
- the "gentle Jesus, meek and mild," preoccupied with lambs
- the hippie Jesus
- the establishment Jesus, clad in red, white, and blue
- the ethnic Jesus—blond and blue-eyed, or black with an Afro
- the out-of-this-world Jesus, a pale ghost floating around

Our challenge is to show both that Jesus Christ is relevant and that he is unique, the mighty Lord from heaven who walked on this earth. It is important that each of us think out honestly and realistically an answer for this question: "If you were not a Christian, would there be anything different about your life?"

I would respond like this:

"In my life, he has been the clue to reality. This is a crazy, mixed-up world, and Jesus Christ helps make sense out of it. He helps me to understand what is wrong with the world and how it can be put back together.

"In my own life, Jesus Christ gives me standards. But he does more than that. I know I fail often. To be able to get a daily, updated forgiveness and fresh power from God when I hurt people or fail by his standards is very important.

"Jesus Christ also helps me experience real self-acceptance. He understands the times when I get down on myself and unconditionally accepts me just as I am. That really helps me become what he wants me to be.

"Also, he helps me to be more interested in others than in building the kingdom of Leighton Ford. He gives me the power to love people and to be patient. We've had some critical times of suffering in our family. Our teenage son came very near to dying with a heart problem. At that time, materialistic values didn't seem very important. In that valley, we really came to know what it was to be able to say God was ruling and overruling in all of this. The unknown factor of death is also scary. I really believe because of Jesus' resurrection he holds hope for me. Because of Jesus Christ, my life takes on significance beyond my own personal fears and hopes. He makes me a part of something bigger. I wouldn't exchange for anything the spirit of oneness and support with Christian brothers and sisters.

"A personal relationship with Jesus Christ is not some mystical thing. Even though I can't see him, he is there—just like the air that keeps me alive. The more I turn to him, the more I discover that every part of life takes on a fresh wholeness because of Jesus Christ. He is the one who holds everything together for me."

"Do you really believe Jesus Christ is the only way to God?"

"I am the way. . . . No one comes to the Father except through me" (John 14: 6). Jesus did not say, "No one can believe there is a God" or "be religious" or "live a fairly moral life" without him. But he did say, "No one comes to the Father."

Almost all religions have elements of truth and some excellent moral teachings. Match a hundred non-Christians against a hundred Christians, and you would find some of the non-Christians morally superior to some of the Christians. So, what is unique about Jesus?

First, he reveals to us God as Father. We can know there is a God, a power, a spirit, a great "something somewhere." But Jesus Christ has focused God personally as the Father who cares for us.

Furthermore, Jesus Christ makes it possible to *come* to the Father in a personal relationship. Christians, Buddhists, Hindus, Muslims, agnostics—all are conscious of moral failures. Jesus' death makes it possible for those who have sinned to come back into the presence of a holy Father without condemnation. Christianity is not unique because of its rituals, institutions, and ethical standards. Christianity is unique in that it tells us about a God who has actually come to this earth to die for us in order that we might come back to him.

"But are his claims true?"

Os Guiness has suggested that we need to understand both that God's truth is the answer, and God's answer is the truth.

The fact that Christianity is true, really true, is something the seeking person must be confronted with. We may start with felt needs, but if conversion to Christ is to be genuine and lasting, it has to involve this issue of truth.

Why is this important? Because the minds of most people today are not at all geared to the idea of truth that is really true. So we have the following variations:

"Truth is relative." In talking with someone about Jesus Christ, we frequently hear, "Well, that's your idea. You have the right to your belief and I have the right to mine. After all, everything is relative." Or, "Well, God may be absolute, but any idea we have of God is relative."

"Truth is psychological." Closely allied is the idea that all truth is just based on our psychological needs. If a Christian believes in God, it is simply because he projects the great cosmic Father to provide a father image for his security. The public is swayed today not by arguments about truth but by advertising that plays on their fears and insecurities.

"Truth is what works." This is the pragmatic argument. We don't ask whether something is true or false but whether it is useful or not.

"Truth is consensus." In *The Christian Mind,* Harry Blamires discusses how the idea of a Christian body of truth is foreign to the secular mind. "Ours is an age to which conclusions are arrived at by distributing questionnaires to a cross-section of the population or by holding a microphone before the lips of casually selected passers-by on the street."[2] Audience ratings and best-sellers determine truth for most people, not the idea of any objective truth outside our own opinions.

"Truth is new." A recently coined word is *neophiliac*—a lover of what is new. In *Future Shock* Alvin Toffler reminded us that in 1784 the first mail coach went ten miles per hour. By the 1880s locomotives reached the enormous speed of 100 m.p.h. Fifty-eight years later pilots were cracking the 400 m.p.h. limit. In twenty years that speed limit was doubled. In our generation, astronauts have circled the earth at 18,000 m.p.h. Living through such vastly accelerated change, people are likely to say, "The world I live in is as different from the one in which I was born as that was from Julius Caesar's. How can you expect me to believe statements in a Bible written 2,000 years ago?"

The sum total of these views is: "Truth is not fixed and final; it is relative to my age, circumstances, culture, feelings, and personal prejudices."

With this mind-set, how do we establish the truth claim of Christ?

First, we have to admit that relativity is true, within limits! We all see things from our own perspective. We Christians do not say *our ideas* of God or the Bible are absolute. The Bible itself was written over hundreds of years in different historical and cultural situations. Accordingly it contains various emphases, styles, and kinds of writings. This does not, however, imply that its message is ever out-of-date or untrue.

Second, we point out a logical inconsistency: if *everything* is relative, that includes the statement "Everything is relative"! The statement thus becomes meaningless. If everything is relative, then communication is nonsense.

Third, we have to be clear that there is a vast difference between Christian truth and the modern ideas of truth described above. Christian truth is not discovered by personal feelings or decided by a majority vote. God's truth is God's revelation. We receive and discover it; we don't make it up. This does not mean that Christian truth is merely a set of propositions and statements. Ultimately, truth is both propositional and personal. Jesus himself said, "I am . . . the truth" (John 14: 6). He also said, "You will know the truth, and the truth will set you free" (John 8: 32).

Some possible objections we may meet at this point are:

"You just believe in Christianity because you have been brought up to need a kind of spiritual security blanket." But this argument boomerangs. I can answer, "The reason you think I believe what I believe because of my early upbringing is because of your early upbringing! You've been taught to presuppose certain things about Christians."

Experience doesn't prove or disprove Christianity. Someone may have become a Christian because he needed a crutch or saw "God" on a drug trip, but that doesn't prove or disprove the truth. In the end, we believe in Jesus not just because he is making a difference in our feelings and experience but because there is historical evidence for him.

"But if you believe something hard enough, that makes it true for you." Paul Little gives an illustration that helps to meet this objection:

A professor in semantics from the University of California, in Berkeley, recently attended a series of meetings where I was a speaker. He was a complete relativist in his thinking. . . . He advanced the popular idea that what we believe is true to us but not necessarily true for other people, and he used this illustration: A man may be tied on a railroad track in a fraternity hazing. When the train whizzes by on the next track, he dies of a heart attack because he does not know that it is not on his track. As far as he is concerned, the train might as well have been on the first track. He believed it was and so it became true for him. You see, what is truth for you may not be true for me. Time and time again we tried to show this professor the significant difference in Christianity, the fact of the resurrection. About the fourth time around the penny dropped. Standing at the blackboard with a piece of chalk in his hand, he suddenly stopped in the middle of a sentence and said, "Hum . . . yes, that would make quite a difference," and sat down.[3]

"As a Christian, you base everything on the Bible as the inspired Word of God. But I don't believe that." Fortunately we don't have to argue in a circle. We can reply, "You don't have to begin by believing that the Bible is the inspired Word of God. All I'm asking you to do at this point is to accept the Bible as reliable history. As such, it claims to tell us what God has done and said for us in Jesus Christ." To establish this, it is helpful to know the basic facts on which we establish the historical reliability of Scripture. I suggest, for example, reading *The New Testament Documents: Are They Reliable?* by F. F. Bruce (InterVarsity).

Often people will say that the New Testament accounts were written so long after Jesus that we can't be sure we have the facts. But that does not stand up. We still have more than four hundred Greek manuscripts of the New Testament. We have papyrus copies of all four Gospels from before A.D. 200. One fragment of the Gospel of John dates back to around A.D. 125. More recently we have heard that part of the Gospel of Mark may be included in certain Dead Sea scrolls written within two decades after Jesus.

Consider the contrast with other ancient writings. The oldest existing manuscript of the writings of the historian Thucydides dates fifteen hundred years after his time. The earliest copies of the writings of Tacitus are eight hundred years after his time. Yet scholars accept their writings. Why should we not accept the New Testament?

Based on the New Testament writings, I suggest that we ought to confront people with two basic questions:

1. *Who was Jesus Christ?* He taught with authority, he accepted worship, he claimed the right to forgive sins, he said he had no sin, he claimed a special relationship with the Father ("I and the Father are one"—John 10: 30) and that his death would make forgiveness possible. There is no parallel. Other great religious leaders told men, "Go to God." Jesus said, "Come to me." In the face of these claims, there are only four options:

- Was he a liar?
- Was he a lunatic who naively believed untrue things about himself?
- Was he legendary, the creation of others (in which case the inventors would be more astonishing than he was)?
- Or was he in truth the Lord from heaven?

2. *How do we explain Jesus' resurrection?* His claims puzzled his disciples too during his lifetime. Then suddenly the central piece fell into the puzzle with his resurrection. Seven weeks after Jesus had died, his followers went out in Jerusalem and said Jesus had appeared to them alive. These men criss-crossed the Roman Empire telling people everywhere the story of Jesus. They met hostility, were imprisoned, beaten, and martyred (the same men who had fled when Jesus was arrested!). When they were threatened, they said, "We cannot help speaking about what we have seen and heard" (Acts 4: 20).

What changed them?

They said it was Jesus Christ appearing to them alive. The very existence and growth of early Christianity is based on the fact that people claimed the tomb was empty. It is very important that we challenge people to think through the alternatives, examine the evidence, and discover that Christianity is based not on the straws of public opinion but on the hard facts of history. (For further study of the reliability of the New Testament, the claims of Jesus Christ, and the grounds for believing in his resurrection, see C. S. Lewis's *The Case For Christianity*, Paul Little's *Know Why You Believe*, and Michael Green's *Runaway World.)*

Of course it is important to understand that we are not trying to "prove" Christianity. The Scripture plainly says, "Without faith it is impossible to please God, because anyone who comes to him must believe that he exists and that he rewards those who earnestly seek him" (Heb. 11: 6). We don't argue people into faith. Faith is a gift that comes to people as they hear the Word of God. The point is that faith is not a blind leap of psychological will power. Faith is a commitment based on evidence.

1.   Francis Schaeffer, *The God Who Is There* (Downers Grove, Ill.: InterVarsity, 1968).

2.   Harry Blamires, *The Christian Mind* (Society for the Propagation of Christian Knowledge, 1963), p. 106.

3.   Little, *How to Give Away Your Faith*, p. 78.

DATE DUE